MATTHEW J BANDOO

Earth Realm

Home Of The Mentally iLL

Copyright © 2025 by Matthew J Bandoo

All rights reserved. No part of this publication may be reproduced, stored or transmitted in any form or by any means, electronic, mechanical, photocopying, recording, scanning, or otherwise without written permission from the publisher. It is illegal to copy this book, post it to a website, or distribute it by any other means without permission.

First edition

This book was professionally typeset on Reedsy.
Find out more at reedsy.com

Contents

Preface

Earth Realm: Home of the Mentally Ill

Earth Realm: Home of the Mentally Ill, a metaphorical term for our societal construct.

Imagine waking up one day to discover that the world you've been navigating isn't real. It's a carefully constructed illusion, a facade so convincing that even your most profound thoughts are its puppets. Welcome to Earth Realm, where the lines between sanity and madness blur, and the only thing scarier than the world outside is the truth within.

Introduction:

Welcome to *Earth Realm: Home of the Mentally Ill,* where we dig deep into the raw reality of the human mind, its vulnerabilities, its complexities, and the influences that shape it. Our minds are delicate, easily moulded by the world's pressures, yet they hold an astonishing depth. We're constantly bombarded with some overt, sneaky programming that skews how we see and interact with life.

We live in a world coated in a deceptive gloss of politics, religious dogma, cultural norms, and ethnic labels. Amid this facade, have we lost sight of who we really are? Are we simply following the script written for us, or are we daring to explore the uncharted depths of our true selves?

In this book, we'll rip away the veneer and get real about how Western ideas warp our sense of normalcy. We'll confront whether we're awake or just drifting through life, accepting whatever's handed to us.

Our journey will also delve into how our early years, from birth to age seven, shape the beliefs and patterns that drive us. This isn't just about observing the world. It's about rolling up your sleeves and delving into the dirt of your own mind. It's about questioning everything you've been taught, reconnecting with your true self, and confronting the raw truths that lie within.

I'll be infusing R.A.P. (Rhythm and Poetry) throughout the narrative to guide us through this exploration. These rhythmic and poetic elements will punctuate our journey, offering sharp, evocative insights that cut through the noise and speak directly to the heart, enhancing the emotional and intellectual impact of our exploration.

So, I challenge you. I respect the time and effort you're investing in this journey. Are you ready to smash through the mirrored illusion that's clouded your view of reality? Can you confront your thoughts and perceptions with brutal honesty and truth? Join me as we unravel the dark, tangled threads of your mind, heart, and spirit and explore how they intertwine with the world around you, shaping everything you think you know.

Purpose and Goals:

Earth Realm: Home of the Mentally Ill is more than just a deep dive into the complexities of the human mind. It's an invitation to question everything you thought you knew about yourself and the world around you. This book aims to unravel the intricate web of external influences that shape our perceptions and behaviours, exposing how these forces can distort our reality and keep us trapped in a cycle of self-deception.

Through this exploration, you'll understand how societal constructs, from politics and religion to cultural norms and ethnic identities, mould our minds and beliefs. We aim to shed light on the often-hidden mechanisms that drive our responses and interactions, helping you break free from the superficial layers of your existence.

Our goals are to Challenge Your Perceptions:

- **Encourage you to question** The "truths" you've been taught and explore the authenticity of your thoughts and feelings.
- **Examine Early Influences:** Show how the programming received in your formative years influences your current mindset and behaviour.

Encourage Self-Discovery: This is not just a journey of introspection but a powerful tool for aligning your inner self with your outer reality. It's about fostering a deeper connection with your true essence, empowering you to live a more authentic life. By the end of this book, you'll have a heightened awareness of how your mind has been shaped and practical insights into reclaiming control over your perceptions and living with greater authenticity. Prepare to confront uncomfortable truths and embark on a path toward genuine self-understanding.

Acknowledgments

I

Part One

1

Painting The Human Experience

Focus:

This chapter explores life's purpose, the human journey, and Earth as a spiritual growth arena.

Transmissions From Earth Realm:

- *"Life is like a wide-open canvas, and every moment we add our unique colours to it..."*
- *"Have you ever thought about how we're like sparks in a cosmic fire, just brief flashes in this huge universe?"*
- *"We're multidimensional beings navigating this intricate mess of existence, spiritual entities living in what I like to call our 'earth suits.' These 'earth suits' are our physical bodies, the vessels through which we experience life on Earth."*
- *"What is Earth, really? Some days, it feels like a cosmic roller-coaster that never stops..."*
- *"Think of Earth as the ultimate playground for the soul..."*

- *"When you zoom out, the planet's biosphere, the thin layer of life on its surface, acts like Earth's skin..."*

Life is filled with contrasts: light and shadow, joy and sorrow. These contrasts uncover the depth of our existence, reminding us that every masterpiece is created with both vibrant colours and the haunting strokes of darkness. These contrasts, the light and the shadow, the joy and the sorrow, add richness and depth to our human experience, which we should appreciate and cherish.

The Human Life – What's Our Purpose?

Have you ever considered how we're like sparks in a cosmic fire, just brief flashes in this vast universe? Inside each of us is a universe full of depth and mystery. We may feel small against the stars, but that tiny flicker carries so much potential.

Life is like a wide-open canvas and every moment we're adding our unique colours to it. The highs, the lows, and everything in between all shape the masterpiece we leave behind, capturing what it really means to be human. When we look at life through this cosmic lens, it hits us: we're both tiny specks and infinite beings. This 'cosmic lens' is a perspective that considers the vastness of the universe and our place in it, which can be both humbling and empowering. It's humbling but also kinda empowering when you think about it. Every experience matters. So, why not paint boldly and embrace our journeys? Let's reflect on the beautiful chaos of existence.

I've always felt we share a common purpose wrapped up in our individual stories. We're not just here to exist; we're here to learn, grow, and explore our own paths. Just like no two fingerprints are the same, our journeys are uniquely ours. Life unfolds like a vast, interconnected web filled with experiences and opportunities. We're all part of this intricate mess of existence, spiritual entities living in what I like to call our "earth suits." This interconnectedness makes us feel a sense of unity and belonging in this vast universe.

When I think about our souls, I picture them nestled in the pineal gland, like the control centre of a spaceship, picking up signals from some higher source like a cosmic radio. This 'cosmic radio' is a metaphor for our connection to a higher consciousness or spiritual realm, guiding us through life's ups and downs. The choices we make and the thoughts we entertain come from this deep, unseen link to something greater.

Think about the simple act of touching a tree. Getting into the texture of the bark, the coolness against your skin, the scent in the air. Each sensation can take you back to a memory, maybe a childhood park or a peaceful hike in the woods. Our minds are like filing cabinets, storing every little detail. On a deeper level, these experiences become part of who we are, right down to our cells. Even sounds have this crazy power; a particular song can zap you back to a vivid moment, like cruising on a sunny afternoon with that same tune blasting in the background. It's wild how something as simple as a song or a touch can spark emotions and memories, shaping the story we carry through life.

Most of us believe we exist in just three dimensions of space, with time considered the fourth dimension. However, physics, particularly string theory and M-theory, suggests as many as 11 dimensions could exist. It can be challenging to grasp. We cannot see or feel these extra dimensions because they are thought to be "compacted," meaning they are folded up so tightly at tiny scales that they are invisible to us. Scientists typically focus on models with 10 or 11 dimensions since anything beyond that becomes mathematically unpredictable. Nonetheless, it's fascinating to consider that there may be entire aspects of reality yet to be discovered.

I've always found comfort in the idea that when our time in these "earth suits" ends, it doesn't mean the end of our story. Energy doesn't just disappear; it transitions. So when our bodies reach their expiration date, our consciousness shifts to a higher dimension, like switching to a new frequency. This thought adds beautiful depth to life, making it feel more meaningful. I used to wrestle with the question: "Is this all there is? Just eat, sleep, shit, and die?" But seeing our spirits as energy changed everything for me. We're more than just flesh and bone; we're eternal beings, and our earthly existence is just one chapter in a much bigger story.

Then there's the multiverse concept. Have you heard about that? Scientists are starting to think our universe might just be one of many. Imagine the implications! Entire realities could exist, each with stars, planets, and rules. Hollywood has been fascinated with this idea for years. Classic examples include The Matrix, which explores simulated realities; Timecop, where changes in the past create alternate timelines; and Back to the Future Part II, with its branching realities. Recently, movies like Everything Everywhere All At Once have taken the multiverse concept to dazzling, mind-bending new heights. It's dizzying yet reflects the immense depth still waiting for us to discover.

But here we are, grounded in the present, in this earthly realm. Even if our spirits have wandered through other lives and dimensions, we focus on this moment. It's like we arrive on Earth with a kind of cosmic amnesia, our past lives hidden from our conscious memory, but there's an inherent awareness that we're more than what we seem. Those past experiences aren't lost; they linger in what some call the Akashic records. Even if we can't consciously recall them, they shape who we are today. Every life lived and every experience faced adds to the mosaic of our existence. We are eternal beings; our journey on Earth is just one thread in a much larger story.

So, what's the ultimate purpose of all this? It's about living fully, loving deeply, and embracing every part of the experience. Every joy, every struggle, every lesson is part of the grand design. We're here to create, grow, and connect with one another. And when our time in these "earth suits" ends, we'll move on to the next phase, continuing our journey in ways we can't imagine. Life, in all its dimensions, is a gift, and I believe that's the essence of our purpose: to live it, to feel it, and to leave our mark on this cosmic canvas.

> *"Earth, man. What a shit-hole."* - ***Alien: Resurrection (1997)***

Earth as a Learning Ground: What on Earth is Earth?

This blunt quote from Alien: Resurrection (1997) makes you think. What is Earth, really? Some days, it feels like a never-ending cosmic roller-coaster, a wild boarding school where we're all just students trying to pass the next test. Consider this: we land on Earth through our mothers, who act as quantum portals connecting us from the spirit world to the physical realm. It's a trippy concept. We get zipped from one dimension to another, and then, BAM! - we wake up in a body, ready to experience life in a whole new way. It reminds me of that 80s series Quantum Leap; there is so much truth to that.

Before our grand entrance here, we float in the spirit realm, surrounded by light and pure consciousness. Picture it: a serene sea of wisdom and peace. But to step into this world, we must incarnate, jumping into these avatar bodies through the portal of our mother's womb. It's akin to downloading ourselves into a brand-new game with infinitely higher stakes. The mother is the gateway, allowing us to transition from that spirit form into a flesh-and-blood existence. And when we're born, it's like opening a new book, yet we carry pages from the last one. All those past lives, traumas, lessons, and talents don't just vanish; they're part of the baggage we bring along, whether we remember them or not.

The wildest part? Life is merely a continuation. We pick up where we left off, even if this new version of us has no clue about the old chapters.

Think of Earth as the ultimate playground for the soul. Here, we learn, grow, and engage in real-world experiences. Relationships, emotions, and challenges form the curriculum. In the spirit realm, you're pure energy and then some, but down here, we have these avatar bodies that enable us to feel, taste, touch, smell, and hear the world around us.

Every experience shapes us and teaches us something new, making us actors on this grand stage called life. But let's not sugar coat it; being trapped in a body comes with its limitations. We have to contend with the ego, fears, and pain, all of which can cloud our perception and obscure the fact that we're immortal souls playing this human game deep down. The journey here is about awakening to that truth and realizing we are more than just these physical shells.

When the time comes to leave this avatar behind, and our bodies finally call it quits, our souls head back to the spirit world. But don't be fooled; this isn't the end. We carry all our lessons, karmic bonds, and energy with us. And the cycle continues; we'll be back. It's like cosmic semesters. Each lifetime is a class, and we return to 'Earth School' until we've learned all our lessons. This ongoing process is about growth, healing, and rediscovering the love and wisdom within us.

Now, let's flip our perspective on Earth a bit. What if it's not just a rock floating in space? What if Earth is alive, conscious, and breathing like us? Imagine it as a giant organism, where everything from the trees to oceans to humans work together like cells in a body. This is where the Gaia hypothesis comes into play, suggesting that Earth isn't merely a passive stage for life but an active participant. Its ecosystems, weather patterns, and life forms interact in ways that keep everything balanced and thriving. When you zoom out, the planet's biosphere, the thin layer of life on its surface, acts like Earth's skin. Just as our skin protects and nourishes us, Earth's ecosystems constantly communicate, striving to maintain equilibrium. When one part suffers, the entire system feels it. Disrupting nature is like giving Earth a nasty rash; ultimately, we are the ones who feel the effects.

Consider that consciousness isn't solely a human trait confined to our brains. What if it's present in everything? From the tiniest microbe to the tallest tree, everything on Earth might possess its own kind of awareness that is different from ours, but awareness nonetheless. Imagine if all of nature is thinking, feeling, and living, just like we do, albeit in its own way. If that's true, we're all part of Earth's vast brain, each contributing to the overall intelligence of our planet. Since we're interconnected, we're harming ourselves when we harm the Earth. Every tree we cut down and every river we pollute is like stabbing a nerve in this massive living brain we're all part of. It's no wonder indigenous cultures have long viewed humans as caretakers of the Earth rather than its owners. Our role here? We must live in harmony with this giant, conscious organism we call home.

Every action has a consequence. When we act mindlessly, we disrupt the balance of life, not just on a personal level but on a planetary scale. The Earth, with all its life forms and energy systems, resembles a grand dance of creation, and we humans are merely one of many dancers. We can either keep the rhythm or trip up the whole performance. The more we respect the Earth and strive to live in harmony, the more we tap into its profound wisdom and understanding. It's all interconnected; ***we are Earth, and Earth is us.***

2

Past Lives, Karma, and Inner Alignment

Focus:

This chapter explores spiritual growth through past lives, karmic cycles, and finding balance within ourselves.

Transmissions From Earth Realm:

- *"Our souls carry echoes of past lives. To explore these realms unveils timeless truths guiding us home."*
- *"Aisha learned she had lived before, as a singer in 18th-century New Orleans..."*
- *"Life isn't merely a sprint from birth to death; it's a marathon spanning multiple existences."*
- *"Karma is like the universe's ultimate balancing act. Whatever we send into the world inevitably comes back like a boomerang."*
- *"Let's dive into something profound: the idea that we are more than just thinking minds..."*

- *"We often poison ourselves mentally, emotionally, and spiritually by holding onto negativity, anger, and fear."*

> *"Our souls carry echoes of past lives. To explore these realms unveils timeless truths guiding us home."* – ***By the Author***

Past Lives and Beyond: Old Souls & Past Life Regression

Imagine a girl named Aisha. From the moment she could speak, she could also sing, **not just your average kid humming a nursery rhyme**, but with a voice that could make you pause and think, "Where did that come from?" Her talent seemed to transcend her years as if she had been practising for lifetimes. Yet, despite her loving home, a shadow of sadness and anxiety loomed over her, a mystery no one could decode.

Then came a pivotal moment, a past life regression session that changed everything for Aisha. She learned she had lived before as a singer in 18th-century New Orleans. But here's the tragic twist: she was born into slavery. In that life, her voice wasn't just a gift but a tool to entertain the people who ripped her from her family. **Imagine the heartbreak of using your greatest talent to entertain those who own you.** The trauma of that existence being auctioned off like cattle, separated from loved ones, and singing for survival left an indelible mark on her soul. Despite the pain, the power of past life regression allowed Aisha to understand and heal from her past, inspiring hope and transformation.

Even though Aisha didn't consciously remember that life, her soul retained the memory. That talent she possessed? A remnant of who she once was. But so was the deep-rooted grief, an unshakable sadness and anxiety that haunted her from childhood. These feelings weren't random; they echoed the pain and oppression of her past life. This illustrates how past life experiences work: we carry not just our skills and strengths but our scars and wounds, too. Aisha's story reminds us that the things we excel at, struggle with, or find puzzling may have roots deeper than we realize. It's as if we're all lugging around invisible suitcases filled with memories, talents, traumas, and lessons from lives we can't consciously recall. This interconnectedness of our past lives and present struggles makes us feel connected and understood.

And it's not just individual souls who bear this burden. Past life traumas can ripple through generations, especially concerning collective experiences like slavery, war, or systemic oppression. **Consider this**: the trauma of slavery didn't vanish with the abolition of physical chains. Emotional chains? They were passed down. When discussing racism and inequality today, it's not just a political issue; for many, the pain is embedded in the soul, carried across lifetimes.

Looking at life through the lens of past lives gives us a fresh perspective on our talents and struggles. Life isn't merely a sprint from birth to death; it's a marathon spanning multiple existences. The soul is on a long journey, with Earth as just one pit stop, a place to address karmic baggage, heal old wounds, and rediscover our true selves. But here's the catch: if we don't learn our lessons, they keep coming back. **The universe hits 'repeat' until we finally get it right.** Ever notice how the same problems recur in your life or across society? That's karma at work. Life is a teacher; if we're not paying attention, those lessons will reappear in this life or the next. It's like cosmic déjà vu.

Humanity isn't exempt, either. Think about the patterns we observe: wars, greed, inequality. If we fail to correct our mistakes, we're doomed to repeat them, lifetime after lifetime. This isn't just a spiritual theory; it's the reality we live daily. The fascinating part? We hold the power to break these cycles. If we confront our past, be it personal, generational, or societal, and learn from it, we can finally move forward.

So, what does this mean for us, right here, right now? The key to our future lies in our past. Whether grappling with personal struggles, generational trauma, or the messes humanity has collectively created, it all boils down to one thing: understanding the lessons we've been given. **We're not doomed to repeat history if we choose to learn from it.** That's both the gift and the challenge of life. Understanding and learning from our past can shape a better future, empowering us and making us feel responsible for our actions.

The journey is long, my friend. But every step in every lifetime is an opportunity to heal, grow, and remember who we truly are.

What Life Presents

Life has a way of constantly presenting us with opportunities, sometimes disguised as challenges. It's funny how we often find ourselves at a crossroads, staring at choices that can shape our future. We may believe we're guided by our best intentions in those moments. Still, selfish desires, impulsive emotions, or deeply ingrained habits all too often take the wheel. It's like trying to steer a ship through a storm, compass spinning wildly, unsure of the right direction.

We've all been there. We think we've figured it all out, only to find ourselves heading toward something we swore we'd avoid. It's not until later that we reflect that we realize how we ignored that quiet inner voice. The one that knew better, but we weren't ready to listen.

Every decision, whether made impulsively or after endless analysis, sets us on a particular path, like branches on a tree. Some trails lead to growth, while others may force us to turn back and try again. Sometimes, we're so caught up in the moment that we forget we're even making choices. We drift, unaware of the direction we've taken, until it feels too late. But hindsight is a gift, even when it comes with regret.

And here's something we often overlook: our energy and thoughts are like magnets. Suppose we radiate positivity, hope, and love. In that case, it's as if the universe responds in kind, sending opportunities, helpful people, and unexpected blessings. But suppose we're stuck in negativity, fear, or self-doubt. In that case, we tend to attract what we fear most: obstacles, challenges, or bad luck. Life notices when we waver, and it reflects our inner state back to us.

Yet, none of this means we've failed. Life isn't about getting it perfect; it's about progress. Every experience, even those that make us cringe in hindsight, teaches us something. Each decision and each so-called mistake is a lesson in disguise, a stepping stone on our journey. And when we reflect on these moments, we gain the wisdom to choose better next time.

Life, in its wisdom, gives us multiple chances. With every new day, we're offered a cosmic do-over button. The goal isn't to avoid mistakes but to learn from them. With each decision and lesson integrated, we get closer to living in alignment with our soul's purpose. We're all works in progress, and patience with ourselves and with others is key. Life is an ongoing evolution, and each step forward counts, no matter how small.

Just as we can attract negativity through fear, we can also manifest positivity through our intentions and energy. We invite the universe to collaborate when we approach life with optimism and faith. Our dreams and goals draw support from synchronistic opportunities, and the right people show up at the perfect moment.

Of course, not everyone will be on board with our vision. Scepticism, competition, and doubt from others may arise when we're chasing something new. But there's wisdom in protecting our goals during their infancy. It's like planting a seed. We nurture it quietly, allowing it to grow strong before revealing it to the world.

Before entering this life, we agreed to face specific spiritual tests and challenges to push us toward growth. These trials may take the form of trauma, loss, or other hardships that shift our life's direction in ways we couldn't have imagined. In the moment, these experiences can feel overwhelming, even unbearable. But looking back, we often see that these challenges were turning points, guiding us closer to our true purpose.

How we respond to these tests shapes who we are. When faced with hardship, do we lose our integrity or rise to the occasion, guided by our inner moral compass? Every crisis and every tough decision moulds our character. It's like a sword being forged in fire. Each trial strengthens, sharpens, and prepares us for what's next.

Life is like navigating a dense jungle or crossing vast, uncharted oceans. It's full of unexpected twists, dangers, and moments when the path seems unclear. Sometimes, it feels like a surreal adventure, confusing and bizarre, like stepping into a real-life version of Alice in Wonderland. It's easy to feel lost or think the world is working against us in these moments.

But we learn to navigate the chaos with intuition, experience, and wisdom gained from past struggles. Life isn't supposed to be easy, but every hardship, every curveball thrown our way, shapes us into the person we're meant to become.

And that's the beauty of it. Even when life feels overwhelming, we're always evolving. Every step, no matter how difficult, brings us closer to the person our soul is destined to be. So, take a deep breath, trust the journey, and know that even the tough moments are part of the bigger picture. Life constantly presents us with opportunities to grow, and we're always moving forward, whether we realize it or not.

Karma: The Cosmic Balancing Act

Karma, it's like the universe's ultimate balancing act. Whatever we send out into the world inevitably comes back like a boomerang. Every thought, word, and action is a seed planted in the garden of our lives. Whether it grows into something beautiful or something we struggle with is entirely up to us. The universe has a way of keeping score, ensuring that the energy we put out returns to us in kind.

At its essence, karma is about cause and effect. It's like a mirror reflecting back the energy we project. We'll see that reflected in our experiences and relationships if we radiate love, compassion, and kindness. But when we send out anger, negativity, or selfishness, we'll reap that in return. It's not about punishment or reward but rather a natural rhythm that balances the universe.

Karma isn't confined to this life. It stretches across lifetimes, influencing our present circumstances in ways we might not even realize. The karma we've accumulated in past lives plays a role in shaping the situations we face now. Every choice we make today creates new karmic imprints, planting seeds for future experiences. It's a dynamic system, constantly evolving with every decision we make.

But it's not only about our actions. Thoughts and emotions also have power. Ever notice how challenges seem to multiply when you're stuck in a negative mindset? That's because the energy we project, whether positive or negative, draws more of the same into our lives. By focusing on kindness, peace, and compassion, we cultivate seeds that lead to future happiness. Every act of forgiveness, every moment of gratitude, nourishes the karmic garden we're constantly tending.

We're all gardeners, shaping the landscape of our lives. What we plant today will grow tomorrow. The universe maintains balance not through judgment but through the natural flow of energy. Our choices shape the future, and we take responsibility for the world we create by being mindful of our actions and intentions. Karma isn't fixed. It's flexible, ever-evolving with our free will.

Even if we're weighed down by karma from the past, we can constantly shift our trajectory. Through acts of service, wisdom, and deeper self-awareness, we can clear away the heaviness and move toward growth and positive transformation. We're never stuck. Every moment offers the opportunity to turn things around and realign with our highest potential.

Ultimately, karma invites us to live harmoniously with universal truth, love, and integrity principles. When we align with these, life flows. We experience more peace and more joy, and we stop struggling against the current. Karma isn't about luck; it's about the natural consequences of our actions. We're consciously shaping our future when we choose love over fear, kindness over cruelty.

Let's be mindful gardeners of our own lives. The seeds we plant today will shape tomorrow, and the energy we radiate will return to us in this lifetime or the next. By nurturing our karmic garden with intention, we're not just creating a better future for ourselves. Still, we're influencing the world in meaningful, lasting ways.

Aligning Head, Heart, and Gut: Finding Balance Within

> "Don't think, feel." – *Bruce Lee.*

Let's dive into something profound: we are more than just thinking minds. Imagine a trio within you, your head, heart, and gut, each a unique source of wisdom, guiding you toward truth in ways that thinking alone can't reveal. Bruce Lee, the legendary martial artist and philosopher, encouraged us to trust our feelings and instincts rather than get lost in over-thinking. You know that moment when your mind spins with questions like, "How should I act to be polite or professional?" That's your head trying to build a framework of appropriate behaviour, but it often distances us from our authentic selves.

When we lead with feeling, we connect directly with our essence. It's not about wearing a mask or following a script; it's about responding organically to the moment. In relationships or leadership, people can sense when someone is trying too hard to be polite or ethical - it feels forced, like an act. But when we tune into our inner wisdom, our words resonate as genuine. You can feel the difference, can't you?

Western science has traditionally placed the brain in our head on a pedestal as the primary decision-maker. But here's a twist: we have three brains working together: the neural brain in the head, the heart, and the gut-brain. Each of these centres offers its own intelligence. The head handles reason, language, and analysis, but sometimes it overshadows the insights from our heart and gut. The heart processes feelings, empathy, and values, guiding us toward compassionate choices. It helps us consider how our actions impact others. Then there's the gut, which reacts instinctively, picking up on nonverbal cues and subtle energies long before our rational mind even has a chance to weigh in. It's like having an internal radar for danger or nourishment.

Instead of relying solely on the logic of our head-brain, we can tap into the wisdom of our heart and gut. This holistic approach transforms our interactions, especially in relationships. Leading with compassion, informed by gut instincts, often serves us far better than cold logic.

When we integrate the wisdom of our head, heart, and gut, we align ourselves with our highest potential. By merging the strengths of these three centres, we nourish ourselves and contribute positively to the world. Our choices flow from a blend of reason, empathy, and intuition. While our thinking brains evolved to assess threats quickly, today's world demands a more balanced approach. Relying solely on snap judgments can make us mistrust others. It's easy to categorize those who seem different as "the other" and react defensively.

But when we open our hearts, we see our shared humanity beyond surface differences. Empathy softens mental barriers, allowing us to connect with one another, no matter our backgrounds. Leading with kindness and seeking common ground creates the foundation for understanding, not division.

History has shown us that thinking alone won't solve our conflicts. The head tends to divide while the heart unites. When we ignore our interconnectedness, we deepen our suffering. By embracing the wisdom of our hearts and recognizing each other as brothers and sisters, we can create the peace our world so desperately needs. It takes courage to lead with tenderness, to set aside rigid judgments born from overthinking. Love is the eternal truth at the core of every being, and our shared heartbeat can drown out the fearful noise of the mind. Often overlooked, our gut instincts can guide us in ways our minds and hearts might miss.

We find our way home in this dance of head, heart, and gut. Together, they weave a rich tapestry of understanding and compassion, helping us navigate life's complexities with authenticity and grace.

We Make Ourselves Sick

We often poison ourselves mentally, emotionally, and spiritually by holding onto negativity, anger, and fear. We're nurturing a garden of toxic thoughts that slowly eats away at us. The more we feed into rage and anxiety, the more we fracture our inner being, leading ourselves down a path that serves no good. Healing starts by clearing out negativity and consciously choosing forgiveness, compassion, and meaningful pursuits.

Our internal state doesn't just affect us. It ripples outward, impacting everyone around us. Negativity spreads like wildfire, fueled further by mainstream media that thrives on chaos and misinformation. We have a choice: keep ingesting this toxic cycle or seek out clarity, truth, and genuine connection.

The first step is to recognize how we're making ourselves sick individually and collectively. Once we see it, we can actively choose a healthier path rooted in wisdom, humanity, and shared purpose.

Healing society begins with personal responsibility. We must disconnect from harmful distractions, seek truth over fiction, and realign with our highest values. Reclaiming our sense of self starts with acknowledging how we've been conditioned to accept beliefs and behaviours that don't serve us. It requires doing the inner work to rediscover our core identity.

For those willing to take that journey, the next step is embodying the truth we uncover. When we live from a place of authenticity, we inspire others to do the same, especially younger generations. They are often more untouched by societal programming. They can remind us of honesty, openness, and the importance of human connection. By embracing our unique gifts and standing firm in our values, we heal ourselves and light the way for others.

True transformation starts within. Instead of trying to change the world, we must turn inward and confront our inner demons, old traumas, negative habits, and self-limiting beliefs. By nourishing our minds and spirits with positivity, we can begin to live authentically. Practices like meditation can help quiet the mental noise, giving us clarity to see the truth within ourselves.

Facing the darkness inside is challenging but necessary. When we meet our fears head-on, we integrate and heal them. This allows us to make choices aligned with our true selves, not the conditioned versions of us that society has shaped. The more we heal, the more we realize that peace and authenticity come from within, not external validation.

Reclaiming our wholeness means recognizing that we weren't born into toxicity. We were conditioned to absorb it. Over time, fear, conflict, and negativity have been programmed into our subconscious, distorting our perspectives and behaviours. The media feeds this addiction to drama, amplifying our worst instincts.

But underneath all that conditioning is a pure, untainted essence, a light that waits to be rediscovered. We reclaim this light by choosing to detox from the negativity around us. We must mindfully choose what we consume physically, mentally and emotionally. What we see, hear, and engage with shapes our reality, whether we realize it or not.

This journey isn't easy. It requires a holistic approach and a mental, emotional, and spiritual "diet" that helps us reprogram our minds for enlightenment instead of fear. But as we make these changes, layers of conditioning fall away, revealing our true selves. Poor mental health isn't a life sentence; it's often the result of choices we can change. Every day, we have the power to nurture our minds, bodies, and souls, creating a future filled with peace, purpose, and vitality.

The power to heal ourselves and society starts from within.

> *To break free from the cycle, starve what no longer serves you. It's not about fighting fire with fire; it's about stepping back, withholding the fuel, and watching the flame die out.* **No reaction, just silence.** *That's where your real power lies.*

> *Remember:* **where attention goes, energy flows.** *When you stop feeding negativity, you disrupt its rhythm. The old patterns lose their grip, and new possibilities take root in their absence. It's not just about turning the other cheek. It's about turning toward something greater. Don't meet negative energy head-on.* **Step away and create a new algorithm** *that reflects the world you* want *to build, not the one you've been trapped in.*
>
> *In this silence, in this deliberate withdrawal, entirely new worlds emerge.*

II

Part Two

3

The Invisible Chains: How Mind-Jacking Shapes Our Reality

Focus:

This chapter unveils the hidden forces that hijack our minds, trauma, propaganda, and social systems and calls us to awaken, reclaim sovereignty, and remember the sacred power of inner truth.

Transmissions From Earth Realm:

- *"'If you don't control your mind, someone else will.' That isn't just a whisper in the dark. It's a soul cry in a world gone numb."*
- *"They never needed chains. We handed over our freedom the moment we chose comfort over consciousness."*
- *"Mind-jacking is the quiet theft of our divine will, disguised as education, entertainment, tradition. And we forget we were born free."*
- *"Trauma isn't just a wound; it's an energetic virus, quietly*

rewriting the script of our lives until fear becomes the author."

- *"We are kept small on purpose, fed with fear, seduced by distraction, and taught to forget the truth of who we are."*
- *"To awaken is to become dangerous. Not violent or dangerous. Because a mind that remembers itself cannot be controlled."*
- *"The path home begins when we stop performing and start listening to the voice within that was never mind-jacked, only muted."*

Did you know?

1. **Project MKUltra:** During the Cold War, the CIA conducted Project MKUltra, using hypnosis, psychedelics, and torture on people without consent to develop mind control techniques, leading to lasting psychological damage.
2. **Operation Mockingbird:** From the 1950s to the 1970s, the CIA infiltrated American media through Operation Mockingbird, planting stories and funding organizations to manipulate public opinion and spread propaganda.
3. **Military Psychological Operations:** The U.S. military spends over $4 billion annually on recruitment and psychological operations, using video games and films to make military service appealing and influence public attitudes toward enlistment.
4. **Australia's White Australia Policy:** In the early 1900s, Australia forcibly removed Aboriginal children from their families to erase Indigenous culture, causing deep and lasting trauma.

5. **China's Cultural Revolution:** During the 1960s and 1970s, millions were sent to re-education camps during China's Cultural Revolution to enforce loyalty to Mao Zedong's regime through intense ideological training and brutal punishment.

> *"If you don't control your mind, someone else will" –* ***John Allston.***

Unpeeling the Onion: The Painful Truths We Can't Ignore

I've peeled back so many layers of life's onion I've lost count. And just like peeling an onion, the more layers I pull back, the more it stings and hurts my eyes. It starts innocent enough, just a tear or two, a slight bewilderment. Still, it hits you: the burn, the raw pain of uncovering brutal truths that make you want to shut your eyes and pretend you didn't see it. Innocence fades, replaced by a jarring wake-up call of barbaric horrors, spiritual awakenings, and unholy injustices. Life was a lot simpler when I was blind to it all.

Ignorance is bliss until it isn't. Something about being blissfully unaware of the chaos happening beyond your line of sight almost makes life feel bearable. But then reality knocks, and you can't unsee the fact that we're caught in a constant, inescapable battle between good and evil. It's like the universe gave us front-row tickets to this twisted show. A blessing and a curse wrapped up in one because we can't have heaven without hell. Free will? Sure, but it's like being handed two options: align yourself with the good or get swept up in the evil. Ironically, many people with good hearts unknowingly defend what they should be fighting against.

See, there's always a puppet master behind the scenes, the ones we call "gatekeepers." These folks thrive on dominance, pulling strings to maintain their control over wealth, resources, and opportunities, while the rest of us dance to their tune like loyal little marionettes. And that's the real devil in the painting. The master-stroke of mind-jacking. They don't need chains to keep us enslaved; we willingly shackle ourselves to their systems because we can't imagine life without them.

Let's get real: what would we do if this whole system crashed and burned? Where would we go? How would we survive? They've got us so wrapped up in their control that we defend the very thing that's killing us because we believe, deep down, that it's better than chaos. We don't even bother to dream of something better, something truly free, inclusive, and focused on solving the real problems. Nope, instead, we're spoon-fed propaganda, fear, and division. All designed to keep us vibrating at the lowest possible frequency, trapped in spiritual warfare we didn't even sign up for.

Our minds are the battlefield, and everything we consume is weaponized against us. We're being mind-jacked, plain and simple, our identities stolen, beliefs manipulated, and our sense of right and wrong twisted beyond recognition. We're so busy playing their game that we forget we even have our own voices.

And don't get it twisted. This isn't new. Mind-jacking has been going on for centuries. It's a family heirloom passed down through generations of power-hungry elites. If you're not born into it, don't worry. You can still earn your seat at the table if you're willing to be their obedient puppet. Because once you've got a taste of that power, it doesn't matter how ugly the truth is. You'll defend their lies until your dying breath. You'll use your status, media platforms, and whatever it takes to keep the narrative working in your favour, even as the world burns around you.

Hijacked Minds: The Silent Takeover of Our Thoughts

They say, "**The mind is a terrible thing to waste,"** but what if the real problem is that you never had complete control of it in the first place? I call it *mind-jacking,* the ultimate psychological heist. It's not just trauma crashing through your brain like a bull in a china shop, though that's a big part of it. No, this is a full-on takeover, where everything from your deepest fears to government propaganda hijacks your mental operating system.

Think of your brain like a computer. One day, you're running smoothly, handling tasks, processing emotions, and then BAM, something or someone hacks in. It could be trauma from childhood, or maybe it's the constant stream of media headlines shouting fear and division. Suddenly, your thought patterns aren't yours anymore. It's like someone planted a virus, rewiring your brain so negativity and anxiety become the default setting.

This is what happens when the mind gets jacked. Trauma sneaks in and rewires you, so you can't tell a real threat from a phantom one. You're stuck in fight-or-flight mode 24/7, like a constant fire alarm, even when there's no smoke. Over time, the anxiety erodes your ability to function. It's no wonder people turn to extremes just to escape, whether it's drugs, violence, or worse.

And it's not just trauma that's behind the wheel. Let's talk about the bigger players who don't need to sneak in because they've been in control all along. Governments, media, and big corporations have mastered the art of mind-jacking. They craft the narratives that tell you what to fear, who to hate, and what to buy. You think you're making independent choices, but they're pulling the strings.

Look at any authoritarian regime. They don't suppress dissent with brute force; they mind-jack their citizens into believing the lies. Propaganda becomes the truth, censorship suffocates free thought, and before you know it, even the most well-intentioned people are defending the very system that's oppressing them. It's not just individuals getting hijacked; it's the entire society.

Religion can do it, too. Some institutions tell people to ignore their inner compass, outsourcing their morality to someone higher in the hierarchy. You're advised to trust the guru and follow the doctrine without question, and if you step out of line? Doubt isn't just discouraged. It's punished. Suddenly, you're not thinking for yourself anymore, just obeying like a good little follower.

Corporations have figured out the same trick. They exploit every psychological weakness to make sure you're too busy chasing shiny things or swiping on your phone to notice that your independence is slipping away. Mindless consumption is rewarded, critical thinking is suppressed, and any desire for something better is drowned out by whatever product they're pushing next.

Here's the bottom line: whether it's trauma that eats you up from the inside or oppressive systems that chip away at your freedom from the outside, the result is the same. Your mind gets hijacked, leaving you a hollow shell of who you once were. And the worst part? Most people don't even realize it's happening.

Reclaiming our minds isn't just about healing from personal pain. It's a radical defiance against the systems trying to control us. It's about thinking for ourselves, questioning everything, and refusing to let trauma or manipulation decide our fate. Because in a world that thrives on mind-jacking, breaking free is the most dangerous thing you can do.

Broken Bonds: The Collapse of Community Spirit

We're told we're responsible for ourselves and each other, but the reality in neglected neighbourhoods tells a different story. Community centres, once the heart of local life, stand abandoned like tombstones of what used to be. The places that should provide support have become shelters for people experiencing homelessness and drug addiction. The spirit of looking out for one another? Long gone. Instead, it's a free-for-all, with people turning their backs, disgusted, as if stepping over the problem will make it disappear. It's a dog-eat-dog world, and we've learned to blame everything but ourselves on government failures, broken families, and destructive policies. It's all someone else's mess.

What's terrifying is the cruelty we now show each other. A lack of care is so profound that young people, growing up in this chaos, start to see violence as just another part of life. To survive, you join a gang. Blood becomes the only thing you can count on, and your loyalty is to the streets. Territory, honour, survival. The law? Morals? Those are just words washed away by the rise of TikTok trends and YouTube fame. Sure, we're hungry for knowledge, but what kind of knowledge are we after?

Instead of communities united in real solidarity, we see niche online groups run by know-it-alls with no real direction. We govern ourselves in these digital ghettos, rebels without a clue. What's right? What's wrong? It's all blurred. And when emotions get too big to contain, chaos erupts. A cop kills an unarmed Black man, and the streets explode in protests and riots. We're waiting for the next spark to set off the powder keg. We react, but there's no plan. Just rage. A boiling over of everything we've bottled up.

And yet, deep down, we know. We know right from wrong, even if we can't say it in all the fancy political terms. But the truth is, we're lost. We lash out when we see the system abuse us, but by the time we're reacting, it's already too late. We see the tip of the iceberg, but we'll never fathom the darkness below. The system that oppresses us, breaks us, and beats us down is the very thing that criminalizes our response to it. It's a cycle we're stuck in: chronic anxiety, helplessness, and the ever-present question: why should we keep living like this?

Mind-Jacked by the School System: Indoctrination Over Education

Reflecting on my school days, I remember walking through those hallways filled with hope and a sense of potential. But as time went on, it became clear that the promise of education was often overshadowed by a rigid system designed to mould us into compliant citizens. It's like stepping into a factory where creativity gets stamped out, one lesson at a time.

I'll never forget the day a teacher told us to "think outside the box." But the reality was that the box was already drawn, and it was tight. We were handed textbooks filled with selective histories and narratives that shaped our understanding of the world while conveniently leaving out the contributions of those who didn't fit a specific mould. I felt like I was being shown a highlight reel of humanity, missing all the messy bits that truly define us.

This effect is even more pronounced in underprivileged communities. I watched as kids from my neighbourhood, full of talent and ambition, had their confidence systematically stripped away. It's heartbreaking to see young boys and girls, often already wrestling with societal pressures, lose their sense of worth in a system that seems indifferent to their potential. It's as if they were set up for failure before knowing what success looked like.

Then, controversial ideologies are introduced in classrooms that do not consider the families involved. I remember feeling uncomfortable during discussions that felt too loaded for our young minds as if we were guinea pigs in a social experiment. It's disheartening when the institutions meant to guide us seem more focused on moulding us than nurturing our individuality.

Let's face it: Schools have started to resemble prisons more and more. Instead of being places for exploration and growth, they've become controlled environments where the focus shifts to surveillance and discipline. Kids, especially those from low-income backgrounds, navigate a maze of rules that often criminalize their natural curiosity. It's a cold reality where youthful energy is met with suspicion instead of encouragement.

The structure of these schools enforces outdated gender norms, pushing students into predefined roles. Dress codes become shackles, and disciplinary actions sideline those who dare to express their true selves. I've seen classmates punished for simply being themselves, their voices silenced in a system that rewards compliance over authenticity.

The hidden curriculum, the unspoken rules about following orders and not questioning authority, teaches kids to accept the world as it is, not as it could be. It's conditioning that wraps around them like a heavy blanket, stifling their ability to dream beyond the confines of what they've been taught.

At the end of the day, schools should be gateways to discovery and empowerment. Instead, they often act as barriers, pushing students toward conformity and internalized powerlessness. We must confront this reality head-on, challenging the structures holding our children back. We can only pave the way for an education that truly inspires and liberates only by dismantling these barriers.

The Prison System: A Deep Dive into Systematic Oppression

When you look at the prison population, the glaring injustice is brutal to ignore: individuals from lower social classes are disproportionately represented behind bars. It's a bitter reality that those who are already marginalized are often caught in a web of systemic oppression that thrives on their vulnerability. Statistically, people from lower socioeconomic backgrounds are more likely to encounter police scrutiny, often for reasons that are far from justifiable. This isn't a coincidence; it's a deliberate setup to keep the marginalized trapped.

Consider the haunting imagery from Spike Lee's film *Boyz N the Hood*: "They put liquor stores and gun stores on every corner in the hood so we can kill ourselves." This grim reality extends beyond urban streets. It's embedded in the fabric of our society. What began as systemic neglect has morphed into a culture where music can sometimes collude with the forces that seek to undermine us, glorifying materialism while stifling our collective potential. It's not just art; it's a catalyst that breeds toxic egos, jealousy, and a sense of division among ourselves.

Reflecting on the past, the contrast becomes even starker. In eras where community activism thrived, individuals banded together against systemic oppression, fighting for sanity, survival, and liberation. They faced brutal police violence and unprovoked assaults, enduring hardships in their quest for justice. But the government's response was devastating: key leaders were assassinated, and communities were flooded with drugs, a calculated assault on the very foundation of those neighbourhoods.

The aftermath has created a perfect storm that enables society to label the marginalized as troublemakers. Minor offences can lead to long sentences, criminalizing simply trying to survive. The dismantling of independent businesses has stripped these communities of options, forcing them to navigate an unforgiving system that traps them in cycles of debt and incarceration.

The prison system doesn't just lock up individuals; it tears families apart. Fathers, often the breadwinners and role models, are removed from their homes, creating a void that disrupts the development of young people and damages family structures. The plea bargain system serves as another trap: 95% of convictions in the U.S. are based on plea deals. Faced with impossible choices, many plead guilty to crimes they didn't commit, trading years of their lives for a chance at freedom that feels like a mirage.

And let's not forget the absurdity of the legal process itself. When you stand before a white judge and a jury that doesn't reflect your reality, the chances of receiving a fair trial evaporate. The system forces you into a corner where accepting a plea deal becomes the only viable escape from an oppressive sentence.

Many individuals are alienated from their communities, driven by a desire to fit into the power structures that oppress them. This internal struggle breeds a tragic irony: fighting to conform to a fundamentally broken system. Slavery has morphed into a new form of mass incarceration, where the prison system becomes a tool of social control.

The private prison industry exacerbates these issues, profiting from keeping prisons full. Investors don't just want their money back; they want their profits to grow. This often means keeping those from lower socioeconomic backgrounds behind bars. The financial incentives are alarming, with the system designed to perpetuate the cycle of oppression.

Unlike other groups with nations advocating for them abroad, those from lower social classes lack the protection and support that could challenge systemic injustices. If authorities targeted wealthier groups the way they target the marginalized, you can bet there would be a response.

In essence, the prison system is a mechanism of mental and social incarceration. It doesn't dispense justice; it maintains control through collective trauma. The absence of fathers and male role models disrupts future generations. At the same time, biased legal processes mock the very notion of due process.

Those who resist often find themselves targeted, while those seeking justice face militarized backlash. The laws designed to protect everyone are weaponized against those who dare to challenge the status quo.

Yet, the struggle for justice is not in vain. By sharing our stories and connecting our experiences, we can lift ourselves from isolation and push for meaningful reform. An unbroken mind is the greatest threat to the system designed to keep us down. When united, our voices and minds can unlock the cages that confine us, literally and figuratively.

The prison system serves as a stark reminder of the deliberate manipulation that keeps lower social classes disempowered and divided. It's not just about individual misfortunes; it's part of a larger agenda, a calculated effort to maintain control through fear and oppression. Until we recognize and address this systematic manipulation, we will continue to be pawns in a game rigged against us.

The Corporate Conspiracy: How Consumerism Is Hijacking Our Lives

Look beyond the glossy ads and the latest gadgets; you'll find something more insidious. Consumerism, the driving force behind today's capitalism, isn't just about buying stuff. It's a carefully crafted system designed to control our thoughts and behaviours. What looks like a choice is often just a clever trap.

Think about it: every ad you see, and every app you use is part of a strategy to keep you hooked. Marketing and tech companies are experts at exploiting our weaknesses. They create needs you didn't know you had, encouraging us to buy more and more while hiding the actual costs.

Take junk food, for instance. It's engineered to be so addictive that you can't stop eating it, even though it's making you unhealthy. Processed foods are created to override our natural hunger cues, leading us to eat more and feel worse. Or consider social media, which keeps you scrolling and seeking likes while collecting your personal data. These addictive technologies exploit our need for validation and escape, keeping us hooked and constantly seeking more.

Then, there are planned obsolescence products designed to break down just after the warranty expires, ensuring you'll spend more money replacing them. However, the hidden actual costs go beyond the individual experience of consumption. For instance, the cobalt used in our smartphones often comes from mines in the Democratic Republic of the Congo, where child labour is rampant. Children as young as seven are forced to work in hazardous conditions to extract this vital mineral to keep our devices running.

Similarly, our clothes frequently come from sweatshops where workers endure long hours and minimal pay. These factories exploit vulnerable populations, many of whom are trapped in cycles of poverty. This endless cycle isn't just about stuff; it's about how this constant consumption affects us deeper, particularly across different social classes. The pressure to keep up with the latest trends fosters a sense of inadequacy, shifting focus away from meaningful relationships and self-worth.

Moreover, this push for endless consumption diverts attention from the unsustainable use of resources, contributing to environmental damage. Our identities become so tied to brands that questioning our consumption feels like a personal attack, making change even harder.

Consumerism amplifies some of our worst impulses: greed, impatience, and envy. It's like a mental trap that we need to be constantly aware of to escape. Absolute freedom comes from recognizing these traps and making choices that align with our true values. By shifting away from mindless consumption, we can reclaim our sense of fulfilment and positively impact the world. The option to break free is ours, and it starts with seeing through the illusion and taking back control.

Corporate Conformity: The Dark Side of Modern Work Culture

Step into a modern office, and you might feel like you've entered a high-tech prison. Behind the sleek design and promises of career growth lies a grim reality: these workplaces are designed more for control than creativity. The sterile environment, strict hierarchies, and relentless surveillance create a culture of compliance rather than innovation.

In this environment, stepping out of line isn't just frowned upon; it can cost you your job. The constant threat of unemployment enforces a reflexive obedience to authority, stifling independent thought. Productivity algorithms and performance metrics reduce human effort to cold numbers, ignoring the actual value of creative contributions. Without real decision-making power, work becomes a series of meaningless tasks, where long hours and unpaid overtime drain cognitive energy and morale, serving only the company's profit margins.

Corporate propaganda pushes workers to identify with the brand, often at the expense of their personal values and ethics. This indoctrination cultivates a sense of loyalty that can blind employees to the oppressive conditions they endure. The impact of this corporate culture is profound, colonizing minds, suppressing critical thinking, and stifling diverse voices. The atmosphere of fear and control fosters burnout, depression, and a loss of potential. Dissent is often met with gaslighting, where valid criticism is twisted into personal failure, further silencing opposition.

In many corporations, the structure and culture contribute to a cycle of mind-jacking. Enforced obedience is commonplace, as strict hierarchies and the threat of job loss compel employees to follow orders without question, suppressing any independent thought that challenges authority. The surveillance state is prevalent, with technologies like keystroke monitoring and email scanning creating a culture of paranoia, pushing workers to self-censor to avoid repercussions. The lack of autonomy leads to a sense of purposelessness; without control over decision-making, tasks feel deadening and meaningless.

Burnout culture is pervasive, as extended hours, unpaid overtime, and constant availability via technology lead to cognitive fatigue and emotional exhaustion. Employees are treated as interchangeable parts within a rigid system of control, often internalizing blame from toxic management practices, which can lead to psychological trauma and a diminishing of self-esteem and confidence. Emotional repression is another consequence, as rigid professionalism forces workers to suppress their feelings and creativity, reducing them to robotic compliance.

To escape this cycle, we must reimagine work environments as spaces that foster creativity, autonomy, and a shared sense of purpose. True transformation comes when workplaces support mental health and allow individuals to contribute meaningfully.

The Hidden Costs of Belonging

Our desire for connection can often lead us to lose sight of who we are. From childhood, societal and cultural pressures can distort our true selves, making it feel like we're navigating a funhouse mirror maze, each twist leaving us more disoriented.

Manipulators, like narcissists, exploit this vulnerability, using gaslighting and intermittent praise to keep us doubting our reality. Corporations, too, capitalize on our need for belonging, urging conformity with catchy slogans that overshadow our individuality. Have you ever worn a company logo with pride while your inner voice cringed? I know I have.

Even friendships can compromise our authenticity as we prioritize pleasing others. I've laughed at jokes that didn't sit right just to fit in. Social media amplifies this struggle, pushing us to curate idealized versions of ourselves, showing up to parties we never wanted to attend.

These pressures chip away at our identities, leading to exhaustion and disconnection. But there's power in recognizing these manipulative tactics. By standing up for our beliefs even when they are uncomfortable, we create space for genuine freedom. Embracing our true selves has helped me forge deeper connections in my community.

We must celebrate diversity and unity in our relationships to nurture our potential. Connecting over shared values allows honest conversations to flourish.

It's crucial to set boundaries and recognize manipulative behaviours like gaslighting and love-bombing. False tribalism stifles independent thought, especially in the social media age, where the pressure to conform can lead to unhealthy comparisons. The fear of ostracization for differing views often pushes us to self-censor.

By honestly examining our social patterns, we can break free from manipulation and cultivate authentic connections. Let's reclaim our voices and embrace the richness of genuine relationships, where we find acceptance and a profound sense of belonging that honours our true selves.

Breaking Free from Mind-Jacking and Government Control

So, let's get real: "Mind-Jacking" is the sneaky thief of our sanity, thriving in a world where misinformation and division run rampant. It's like a twisted lottery where the odds are stacked against the rest of us while a privileged few bask in the spoils. We're all players in this high-stakes game, stuck in a maze of half-truths and manipulative lies, and our mental health and personal growth take the hit.

We're constantly plugged in, but let's be honest: Our sense

of choice often feels as real as the empty promises of the latest gadget. Life has turned into a mindless cycle of consuming, conforming, and repeating, leaving us feeling stripped of true autonomy. The truth? We're held back by limiting beliefs and fears that keep us chained to a system designed to control us.

When will we shake off this mental bondage? These invisible chains don't just weigh us down; they crush our dreams and twist our aspirations. It's time to take back control of this relentless cycle of exploitation and oppression. We deserve more than being cogs in this machine.

So, what's the game plan? We need to break free from this dark comedy of errors. It starts with reconnecting with our true selves and embracing our core values, stopping the habit of caring too much about what others think. It's not just about finding our purpose; it's about flipping the script written for us by those in power. If we don't stand for something, we risk becoming the punchline in a tragic joke mind-jacked into a life of compliance and mediocrity.

Have we become so comfortable in our ignorance that we've chosen to stay socially dumb, deaf, and blind? Many seem okay, nibbling on a tiny slice of the pie, resigned to the chaos around them. It's easy to think, "What can we do about it?" and then fall into the routine of eating, sleeping, and repeating the same cycle.

But it's time to reject that mindset. We're not just passive characters in a dystopian drama. To break free, we need to question the script, defy the roles handed to us, and dare to imagine a future where freedom and self-determination aren't just illusions. By shedding the shackles of mind-jacking and embracing our authentic selves, we can create a reality where our potential is more than a dream. It's a vibrant, lived experience.

4

Trapped in the Static: The Disconnect of Modern Isolation

Focus:

This chapter explores the silent epidemic of modern disconnection, tracing its roots through digital overload, synthetic consumption, and the engineered noise that steals our presence. It calls us to remember our innate capacity for deep connection, embodied wisdom, and conscious living.

Transmissions From Earth Realm:

- *"We scroll for connection and end up more alone than ever, caught in a loop designed to numb, not nourish."*
- *"Isolation isn't an accident; it's a feature. When you forget your roots, you forget your power."*
- *"We've become shadows of ourselves fed by algorithms, hollowed out by convenience, and addicted to the noise that keeps us from feeling."*

- *"The 'sunken place' isn't fiction. It's where we go when we let the world think for us."*
- *"Low vibrations don't just drain us. They shape us. Fear, anxiety, distraction: all frequencies tuned to keep us in chains."*
- *"Our food is a metaphor: highly processed, stripped of life, easy to swallow but hard to live with."*
- *"This isn't just about food or phones; it's about remembering that we are sacred beings, not products of a system built to keep us asleep."*

Did you know?

1. **Digital Overload and Mental Health Decline:** Research shows that excessive screen time is linked to increased rates of anxiety, depression, and loneliness. Constant exposure to social media and digital notifications can exacerbate feelings of isolation and disconnection, creating a cycle that's hard to break.
2. **Processed Foods and Mental Health:** A growing body of evidence suggests that highly processed foods laden with sugars, artificial additives, and unhealthy fats are linked to worsening mental health conditions. These foods can disrupt brain chemistry and contribute to mood disorders, making emotional struggles even more severe.
3. **Social Media Manipulation:** Studies reveal that social media platforms are engineered to exploit psychological vulnerabilities, leading users to feel inadequate and disconnected. The algorithms that drive these platforms

prioritize engagement over well-being, often amplifying negative emotions and self-comparisons.

4. **The Disconnection Epidemic:** Despite the illusion of constant connectivity, surveys have found that many people report feeling profoundly lonely and isolated. The superficial nature of online interactions often fails to provide the genuine emotional support needed for mental health, leaving many feeling adrift.
5. **Cultural Amnesia:** As modern conveniences and digital distractions dominate our lives, there's a growing loss of cultural and historical awareness. This detachment from our roots and traditions can lead to a sense of purposelessness and identity loss, further deepening the feeling of disconnection from ourselves and our communities.

> *"We are living in a dystopia, in a world dominated by technology and disconnect, alienation, loneliness, and dysfunction." - **Steven Wilson.***

Lost in the Noise: Finding Real Connection in a Distracted World

Have you ever felt like you're drifting through life, surrounded by people but never really *with* them? For anyone battling depression, anxiety, or mood disorders, that feeling is all too familiar. The simple act of being around others can feel like an exhausting performance. Your mind's spinning, racing from one worry to the next, making it hard to stay in the moment even when you want to.

And let's be real: Our world doesn't make it easy for us to

slow down. We're constantly bombarded with noise. It's not just the literal noise of traffic or notifications; it's the endless scrolling, the barrage of perfectly curated lives flashing across our screens. We're overstimulated yet undernourished, our mental health suffering while we crave connection that feels out of reach. We feel isolated in the crowd, and that's a dangerous place to be.

But there's hope. As disconnected as things might feel, the key to finding a real connection with others and ourselves starts with understanding what's pulling us apart. Change is possible, and it begins with us.

We live in a world of distractions that distract us from anything real. Think about it: How many times a day does your phone steal your attention? How often are you chasing fleeting satisfaction that makes you feel even emptier afterwards? From social media's constant demand for our eyes to processed foods that leave us forgetting what real nourishment even feels like, distractions aren't just in our heads; they're built into the fabric of our lives.

But here's the question we must ask ourselves: What have we lost in all this noise? Self-reflection is a powerful tool for regaining control of our lives.

This isn't about bashing technology or blaming modern life for all our problems. It's deeper than that. This is about waking up to how these things have slowly reshaped our minds, bodies, and spirits without us even noticing. We've been cut off, disconnected from ourselves, each other, and the things that matter. And while we're coasting through life in this haze, forces are benefiting from keeping us in this cycle of distraction. For instance, the idea that success is measured by social media likes or that happiness can be found in the next digital purchase are stories we've been fed that have shaped our beliefs and behaviours.

So, how do we break free? It starts by questioning everything. The stories we've been fed and the beliefs we've adopted without a second thought, it's time to look at them with fresh eyes. Our roots, history, and communities are still here, waiting for us to reconnect. There's wisdom in where we come from that can guide us back to what we've lost.

This chapter reflects a journey through the disconnects that have taken over our lives. It's a call to remember who we are, to question who we've become, and to imagine who we could be if we start paying attention again. Because if we don't, the ability to think for ourselves, to live authentically, and to shape our future might slip away for good. But it's not too late. By recognizing the forces that pull us into the sunken place, we can start to reclaim our lives and our minds. We can break free from the cycle of distraction and rediscover the joy of genuine connection and meaningful living.

Into the Sunken Place: Reclaiming Ourselves in a World of Distraction

Ever feel like you're sinking, like no matter how hard you try to stay present, there's this invisible force dragging you down? That's the "sunken place" from *Get Out*, and that metaphor hit home. The main character sinks helplessly while his mind and body are taken over terrifying. But honestly, it's not far off from how many of us feel today. Trapped, distracted, and pulled in a hundred different directions by forces we don't fully understand.

We're spiritual beings trying to survive in a world that keeps us disconnected from that spirit. It's like we're on autopilot, following paths laid out for us by algorithms, by companies who don't care about us, just the data we generate. And as much as we like to think we're in control, are we really? Or are we just getting moulded into versions of ourselves that someone else designed without knowing it?

I've been there. It's that moment when you're scrolling through social media for hours, lost in the feed, and then you snap out of it, like, *wait, where did the time go?* And even worse, what did I gain from all that? Nothing but a mind full of other people's lives and some cheap dopamine hits. It's almost like you're watching your life pass by, but you're stuck on the sidelines, powerless to stop it.

But does it have to be this way? Are we all doomed to be passengers hijacked by distractions?

I don't believe so. If we look back, there was a time when people were more rooted and connected to each other, nature, and their own truths. I'm not saying it was perfect, far from it, but life felt real. People didn't rely on filtered versions of reality to connect. You got your food from the ground and your wisdom from the people around you, not from a data-mining company feeding you what they want you to know. Sure, propaganda existed, but it wasn't drilled into your brain through every screen, every click. There was space to think for yourself, to breathe.

But let's be real: nostalgia can only take us so far. We're not going back to those times. The present is what it is, and it's complex as hell. The noise is everywhere, and we can't just wish it away. But that doesn't mean we must stay lost in the sunken place.

The real power lies in recognizing what's been taken from us and deciding to take it back. You know, reclaiming what's ours.

We still control what we consume, whether the junk they sell us as food or the "information" they try to feed us. The choice is still in our hands. And no matter how disconnected this world tries to make us, human nature hasn't changed. We still crave real connection, fundamental knowledge, and absolute freedom. That's the stuff they can't take from us.

So here we are. The sunken place is real, and it's creeping into our lives. Will we let ourselves be dragged under, lost in distractions, or do we rise? It starts with waking up with awareness. And once we're aware, we've got a choice. We can reclaim our minds, our bodies, our lives. Because if we don't? Well, the future's not looking too bright. The depths may be waiting, but I'm not going down without a fight. What about you?

Frequencies: Tuning Into What Controls Us

Frequencies are everywhere, like ghosts in the machine. They slip into your head without warning, making you feel things and think thoughts that aren't yours. Some frequencies heal. For instance, 528 Hz is said to be connected to DNA repair, tapping into some universal harmony. Life doesn't just flow when you're in sync with that; it aligns. But how often are we really in tune with that kind of energy? Let's be real: most of the time, we're caught in the opposite.

Then there's the darker side. Low frequencies slither through your mind, feeding your fear and dragging you down. Some say that anxiety hums at a lower vibration and fear even lower, around 100 Hz. It's not just an emotion; it's a force. You don't see it coming, but once it's there, it owns you. Everything feels off, like your bones are shaking, and you can't find your balance. It's more than just a feeling it's control. And the worst part?

You don't even know what's pulling the strings.

Music plays a massive role in all of this. It's not just something we listen to; it's a weapon crafted to make us feel what someone else wants us to. Back in the day, people used music for connection and healing. Tribal drums and chants weren't just sounds; they were links to something higher, something raw. They understood that sound wasn't just noise energy connecting you to the earth, ancestors, and truths deeper than words. But now? That connection's been twisted.

Today's music is engineered to drag you under. Heavy bass lines and hypnotic rhythms don't just get stuck in your head; they trap you. You think you're just vibing, but really? You're being pulled along, controlled by frequencies designed to keep you consumed, distracted, and numb. Every beat is a leash, tethering you to something you can't see. We dance to the beat, but who's really in control?

Certain songs can make your skin crawl, yet you can't stop listening. That's by design. The frequencies behind those beats reach your subconscious, flipping switches in ways you can't fully grasp. The highs make you feel free, floating above it all. The lows? They drag you deeper into your own darkness, amplifying your worst fears. Once upon a time, music was a conscious tool. Now? It's a trap.

So, what do we do with this? The game's rigged, but knowing the rules gives you a fighting chance. Awareness is power. Once you see how these frequencies work, you can choose which ones to let in. You don't have to let those low vibrations run your life. You can tune into the frequencies that heal, reminding you of what's real and truly matters.

No one's going to hand you that control. You've got to reclaim it. If you don't, those lower frequencies won't go anywhere.

They'll keep dragging you down, feeding off your fear, until you're so deep that you can't tell which thoughts are yours and which were planted there.

You can stay lost in the noise or tune in to something higher. It's not an easy path, but it's the only real one.

Feeding the Illusion: Breaking Free from the Food Matrix

We rarely stop to question the very foundations of our reality. While it may sound abstract, the implications are efficient. If life is a simulation, if our perception is constantly manipulated, we must scrutinize what we take for granted. Start with something as fundamental as food. If even our daily sustenance is engineered to deceive, what else might be an illusion?

Consider the modern supermarket. Aisles overflowing with items masquerading as food often contain carefully packaged imitations. Processed beyond recognition and filled with chemicals, additives, and lab-grown components, these edible simulations are sold as nourishment but were never intended to sustain human life. Instead of providing essential nutrients, they fill us up while starving our bodies over time, eroding our health from the inside out.

Our bodies are not machines with replaceable parts but living organisms, intricately balanced systems. Consumption of toxins, allergens, and inflammatory foods disrupts this balance. This deterioration doesn't happen overnight, so it often slips under the radar. Look around: Rising rates of autoimmune diseases, infertility, and mental health crises are not isolated incidents; they are symptoms of a system that is out of sync, a body crying out after years of imbalance.

In our busy lives, we've become disconnected from the source of our food. The warning signs are evident, but we're often too distracted to notice. Our biological needs haven't changed, and real food, unprocessed and close to the earth, remains the only proper fuel for our bodies. As we become more aware of the illusion cast by modern food production, we can reclaim control over our health, both mental and physical. Even in a world inundated with disinformation and deception, the power to choose what we consume remains in our hands, and that choice can be transformative.

If our food has become an engineered lie, what else that we consider "real" might be artificial? When our meals deceive us, how can our thoughts not reflect that same falsity? We've become what we eat: cheap, processed, and synthetic. Yet, the mind, dulled by chemical concoctions, still holds the power to awaken.

Convenience often becomes our enemy. Packaged foods marketed as convenient and inexpensive create a false sense of security, making us feel trapped as if there is no alternative. But the truth is, we still possess free will. The question is, are we willing to awaken it?

Sure, there are excuses. Time is short. Healthy food can be perceived as expensive. But these justifications keep us locked in the food matrix, prisoners of our complacency and ignorance. Overfed yet undernourished, we indulge in a cycle of constant snacking, mistakenly believing it's convenient. Yet, every bite of distraction robs us of essential nutrients and minerals, leaving us deficient and sapping our energy. Proper convenience lies in making informed choices and selecting food that nourishes rather than poisons.

We cannot continue sleepwalking, allowing our choices to slowly undermine our well-being. True satiety and fulfilment do not come from chemical hits or convenience foods; they arise from moderation and consuming food close to its source. We risk walking ourselves into an early grave if we remain on this path.

Fortunately, better paths have always existed. All we need to do is open our eyes and start walking.

Slow Suicide Syndrome

I know most of us aren't actively plotting our demise, but let's be honest: many of us are sleepwalking through life, taking the slow road to self-destruction. We're on a long, winding highway to nowhere, and every fast-food burger or hour wasted scrolling through social media adds more miles to our journey. Every poor choice is a pothole, and instead of steering clear, we just hit the gas.

Let's face it: modern life has us on autopilot. We've traded our vitality for the illusion of convenience. Desk jobs, junk food, and mindless binge-watching are like quicksand: easy to get into but hard to escape. Each time we choose the path of least resistance, we chip away at our health and sense of purpose without realizing it. It's a slow burn that leaves us feeling drained and directionless.

Sure, many of us know these habits aren't doing us any favours. Our gut is waving a neon flag, yelling, "Hey! This isn't how you're meant to live!" But here we are, stuck in a loop, hitting snooze on our potential. Knowing better doesn't cut it; applying that knowledge makes a difference. Information is just noise until we turn it into action. Finding your calling is one thing; living it daily is where the magic happens.

But don't throw in the towel just yet. It's never too late to take a detour off that autopilot highway. Start by reclaiming what makes you feel alive: your energy, purpose, and agency. Make daily choices that nourish you, whether savouring a home-cooked meal, getting quality rest, or surrounding yourself with good company. Every step forward, no matter how small, counts. With your eyes open to the pitfalls around you, you're holding the pen to your life's story.

Distractions include relentless marketing images, societal expectations, and political noise, which constantly pulls our attention away from what truly matters, like white noise in the background. We're conditioned to operate on autopilot, reacting to these influences without thinking. It's like we've got a GPS that only leads us in circles, and we can't figure out how to recalibrate.

Remember the days before the internet took over? Life was less chaotic, and we had more time to reflect. By tuning out the "tell-lie-vision" and minimizing those endless broadcasts, we could actually listen to ourselves. We engaged with our education because our options were limited; we focused on mastering the skills that helped us thrive. We gathered around the dinner table, cooking meals from real ingredients and sharing our lives with those we cared about. It felt human, connecting over food and laughter instead of scrolling through screens.

If you're lucky, you can get one home-cooked meal on Sunday. The rest of the week? It's a parade of takeout and microwave dinners. Convenience reigns supreme, but it often steals the very essence of life.

So, let's shake off the shackles of distraction and convenience and challenge ourselves to be more intentional. We owe it to ourselves and those we care about to reclaim our lives, one mindful choice at a time. You've got this; take that first step.

Have Our Minds Been Hijacked by Modern Life?

A nagging question lingers: Have our minds been hijacked by modern life in ways we don't fully grasp? You must be out of your mind if you think we're living our best lives. It's a heavy thought, primarily when I reflect on how previous generations experienced life with more immediacy. They had fewer distractions, more meaningful connections, and those sacred family dinners where the food was authentic and the conversation flowed freely. Time stretched, allowing us to savour moments rather than rush through them like we do now.

Now, we find ourselves tugged in every direction by hypnotic screens and engineered foods that mimic the real deal. The disconnect is palpable; I can feel it deep in my bones, even if I struggle to understand it. It's as if we've been gently nudged away from authentic living by forces that thrive on our attention and consumption. Yet, can we still sense this gap between who we truly are and how we live? That's a glimmer of hope. It means that our genuine selves are buried beneath the noise.

But how do we bridge this chasm between the wisdom of the past and the challenges of our present lives? It starts with open, honest conversations like the one we're having right now. By stepping back and reflecting on just how far we've drifted, we can begin to reclaim our lives. Awakening to this truth isn't a quick fix; it's a slow, winding journey. But as we gather insights, they illuminate the path forward.

The age-old adage "*Know thyself*" resonates now more than ever. Throughout history, this wisdom has echoed across cultures, reminding us of the importance of self-awareness. By reflecting on our past, our histories, our traditions, and our cycles, we can better understand today's dizzying pace of life. Even looking back a few decades offers glimpses of a world less marred by relentless stimulation and distraction.

For many marginalized communities, particularly Indigenous peoples and descendants of Africa, reclaiming history is not just a nostalgic endeavour; it's a necessity. Too often, their full stories have been deliberately obscured, their true essence twisted or forgotten. Yet buried within those lost chapters are profound truths waiting to be rediscovered, truths that restore identity, purpose, and direction.

Know thyself takes on new significance when we reclaim our histories not from a place of oppression but from a standpoint of strength. When we seek our roots as free individuals rather than victims of a system, we reconnect with the wisdom and resilience of our ancestors. This powerful connection grounds us, reminding us of who we are beyond the labels and limitations imposed upon us. From that sense of wholeness, our purpose becomes clearer and our steps more assured.

But truly knowing ourselves requires more than a casual glance at the surface. It calls for a deep dive into the decisions, traditions, and principles that shape who we are as a people. These guiding elements show us how to navigate the future. History isn't just a relic of the past; it's the prologue to our tomorrow. The values and ways of old, those that have withstood the test of time, still hold the answers we seek. They're there, patiently waiting for us to rediscover their relevance in our lives.

As our world spins faster than ever, the pull of history offers balance. It anchors us, providing stability when everything else feels uncertain. The path ahead becomes clear only when we grasp where we began. But it takes courage to seek the truth, especially when today's reality seems so absolute, so inescapable.

It's time for our blinders to fall away. Only then, with eyes wide open to the broader vistas of time, can we reach for the eternal and recognize the way back home. This journey of rediscovery, reconnecting with our roots and authentic selves, is the key to reclaiming our lives from the clutches of modern life.

Finding Connection in a Disconnected World

Feeling like modern life is pulling you away from what really matters? You're not alone; I've been there too. The constant buzz of digital distractions, the overload of processed foods, and the relentless media stream can make it tough to stay grounded. But we can reclaim our sense of presence and purpose with a few intentional steps. Here's how you can start:

1. **Mindful Attention:** *Our devices are designed to grab our attention and never let go. It helps to set firm limits on screen time and make a habit of stepping outside. Whether a walk in the park or just sitting in your backyard, nature helps reset your mind and gives you a break from the digital chaos.*
2. **Critical Consumption:** *Take a good look at what you're consuming, not just food but also news, social media, and ads. I've learned to be more discerning about where I get my information. Seek sources that offer real solutions and align with what you care about rather than just what's trending.*
3. **Real Connections:** *Building genuine relationships has been a game-changer for me. Find communities or groups where you can connect with like-minded people. Share skills, ideas, and*

inspiration. These real-world connections keep us grounded and remind us of what's essential.

4. **Authentic Goals:** *Reflect on what matters beyond societal pressures. I've had to step back and reassess my goals to ensure they align with my deepest values. It's about making your life fit what truly resonates with your soul.*
5. **Practical Skills:** *Learning practical skills has been incredibly fulfilling. Whether cooking a meal from scratch or fixing a leaky faucet, working with your hands helps build confidence and keeps you connected to reality. It's a tangible way to feel accomplished and self-reliant.*
6. **Exercise Your Choice:** *Look for areas where you can opt out of unhealthy systems. Small changes, like choosing more ethical products or reducing reliance on specific technologies, can make a big difference. Every choice you make to live authentically matters.*
7. **Evolve Your Mindset:** *Regularly check in with your beliefs and mindset. Questioning my assumptions and being open to change is crucial for growth. As you learn more about yourself, let those insights guide your journey.*
8. **Compassion and Community:** *Show compassion for yourself and others. We're all navigating this complex and sometimes isolating world. Building a supportive community and offering mutual encouragement can make all the difference.*

5

Caged in Comfort: The Hidden Prisons of Modern Life

Focus:

This chapter powerfully exposes the hidden barriers of contemporary existence, such as processed foods, constant overstimulation, digital isolation, and growing disconnection from nature. It uses the metaphor of incarceration to illustrate how our routines can confine us and challenge our perception of freedom. This compelling narrative calls us to awaken to the reality of our situation and rediscover the vital connection to nature and our own consciousness, urging us to break free from these invisible chains.

Transmissions From Earth Realm:

- *"We mistake comfort for freedom, but numbness is not liberation."*
- *"Your cage might have no bars, but that doesn't mean you're*

free."

- *"A walk in the woods is not escape – it's remembrance."*
- *"Processed food, processed lives – both are stripped of nourishment."*
- *"Nature doesn't shout to be heard. Maybe that's why we've forgotten how to listen."*
- *"The scroll never ends, because it's not meant to let you stop and feel."*
- *"Freedom starts when you stop asking systems for permission to be whole."*

Caged in Comfort: The Hidden Prisons of Modern Life

The U.S. has the highest incarceration rate in the world, with over 2 million people in prisons. This serves as a powerful call to action for advocacy and positive change. Despite the harsh conditions and lack of mental health resources faced by many inmates, there is hope. Over 50% struggle with mental illness, but with the proper support, rehabilitation is not only possible but within reach. Additionally, our everyday choices, like the convenience of processed foods, can affect our health similarly to prison meals. Despite having social media, nearly 60% of people feel increasingly isolated, pointing to a broader issue of loneliness in society. Together, we can foster a kinder, more connected world!

> *"True freedom isn't just about breaking physical chains. It's about freeing the mind from the mental constraints imposed by ourselves and the systems around us."* – ***By the Author.***

Disconnected from Nature: Life as a Prison Cell

We often take the concept of freedom for granted, believing that we are truly free because we can walk through a park, take a vacation, or choose what to eat for dinner. But are we? When we're disconnected from nature, from the rhythms that once grounded us, does life become a cage we don't even see?

Freedom and Prison: Is There a Difference?

The difference between freedom and prison isn't the iron bars. It's the mental and spiritual captivity that separates the two. Nature once offered a connection to something bigger than ourselves, a rhythm, a balance, a place where time was dictated by the sun and moon, not the never-ending ping of notifications. But as we've distanced ourselves from the land, we've confined ourselves in a prison of our own making.

Nature doesn't follow our clock, stress about deadlines, or care about profit margins. Its wisdom is ancient, living in cycles and seasons that turn without our interference. But our modern, urbanized world traps us in routines that do not involve survival, joy, or community. Instead, we become inmates in a system that rewards productivity over purpose.

Think about it: the walls of our lives may not be concrete, but they are still there. We wake up to the same alarms, rush through the same congested streets, work under the same fluorescent lights, and sleep as exhausted as we did the day before. All the while, the natural world outside shrinks in our rearview mirror.

Disconnected from the Natural World

We've engineered a reality where food comes from factories, not fields. Our bodies are sedentary in chairs, staring at screens instead of moving with the earth. And in that disconnect, we lose something crucial: our freedom. Not just freedom of movement but liberty of spirit, freedom from the endless cycle of modern life that feels like a prison in its own way.

The closer we are to nature, the more alive we feel. Yet, the further we drift, our bodies and minds atrophy. Nature can remind us who we are, grounding us in something beyond ourselves. It's so much more than just hiking or vacationing in stunning destinations! Nature truly serves as our most excellent teacher, enlightening us on life's simple and intricate aspects. It offers profound guidance on how to live vibrantly and meaningfully. Embracing these lessons keeps us connected, preventing us from becoming stuck in a life that, while convenient, misses out on genuine fulfilment. Studies have shown that spending time in nature can reduce stress, improve mood, and enhance cognitive function. Let's cherish and learn from the wonders around us!

Modern Life: A Comfortable Prison

In contemporary life, the bars of our prison are invisible, but they exist in every overstimulating advertisement, every piece of processed food, and every hour spent scrolling through endless streams of curated content. We have become so used to this cage that we hardly recognize it anymore. The illusion of freedom, the ability to choose between different brands, shows, and career paths, distracts us from the fact that we're not free. We're choosing between options that have already been selected for us. Some may argue that modern life offers more freedom than ever, with endless opportunities and choices. However, these choices are often constrained by societal norms, economic pressures, and the influence of powerful corporations, leading to a form of 'freedom' that is more akin to a comfortable prison.

Our ancestors knew nature intimately. They understood that living close to the land wasn't just survival but a kind of liberation. Though they faced challenges, their lives were intertwined in a way we're beginning to overlook. Nature's unpredictability added excitement and depth to life's journey! While we may not have certainty, that uncertainty offers us true freedom. Today, let's embrace the adventurous spirit instead of settling for comfort. After all, comfort can be misleading! Too much comfort becomes complacency, and that complacency is what locks us into our daily routines without even realizing the cell door has been closed.

But here's the thing: just because you're in the prison of modern life doesn't mean you can't break out. The key is still hidden in plain sight, waiting for us to remember where we left it. The key is reconnection. I remember feeling trapped in the routine of modern life, but a simple walk in the woods opened my eyes to the beauty and freedom of nature. Reconnecting with nature is not just an option; it's a necessity. It's not about running off to the woods to live in a cabin, though that may sound appealing. It's about paying attention to the natural world however you can.

Reconnecting with nature can start small. It's not about running off to the woods to live in a cabin, though that may sound appealing. It's about paying attention to the natural world however you can. Start with the food you eat. Where does it come from? How does it nourish you? Take time to notice the trees, the sky, the wind, and the seasons changing around you. For instance, you can start a small herb garden in your kitchen, walk in a local park during your lunch break, or simply sit outside and observe the changing sky. You can also plan a weekend camping trip, visit a local farm, or volunteer for a conservation project in your community.

Nature is resilient, and so are we. Even amid modern life's confinement, we can return to that deep well of wisdom that has always been there. We just have to slow down and remember that nature doesn't need us, but we need nature. Without it, life can feel stifling. But here's the excellent news: freedom is a choice we can all embrace! It's not merely influenced by our surroundings but by our mindset. Even in our fast-paced, technology-driven lives, we can take a moment to reconnect. Let's step outside, take a deep breath, and remind ourselves that we belong to something much greater than the hustle of modern life. The power to choose freedom is always in our hands!

The prison of disconnection only holds us as long as we accept it. The moment we step outside, touch the earth, and reclaim our place in the natural order, we are free. The world may not change overnight, but the shift happens within. The difference between freedom and prison is not the bars. It's the mindset.

True freedom is not just about the absence of constraints; it's about our incredible ability to choose how we navigate and thrive within them!

Inside the Walls: Navigating the Mental Health Maze Behind Bars

Have you ever paused to think about what life is truly like behind bars? It goes beyond steel and concrete; it's a dynamic mental journey within those walls. When you're incarcerated, the experience transforms into an intense battleground for your mind, challenging your resilience in ways you might never have expected.

The Weight of Isolation: Mental Health Challenges

Visualize being in a place where each day eerily resembles the last, and your world is confined to a narrow view or fleeting phone calls. This kind of isolation poses significant challenges - not only to your physical health but also to your mental well-being. It's like existing in a perpetual twilight zone, where time can feel static, and feelings of self-worth can dim. The looming threat of violence and the limited personal space can diminish your spirit and cloud your Reality. This continuous psychological grind chips away at your confidence and clarity, making it an uphill daily battle.

Rehabilitation or Retaliation? The Struggle to Reintegrate

The journey towards rehabilitation goes far beyond just attending programs and classes; it's about actively confronting and overcoming the haunting echoes of trauma and anxiety that linger long after release. How do you begin to envision a bright new life when past shadows still seem to loom? Yet, with determination and support, the potential for a fulfilling future awaits! The struggle is real; rebuilding your life while managing deep-seated mental scars is like trying to build a house on a shaky foundation. Many of us find ourselves stuck in a cycle where the prison environment has already set us up for failure, even before we step back into society.

From Locked Cells to Open Roads: Embracing New Beginnings

Reintegration is more than just stepping back into a job or reconnecting with family; it's an incredible journey that involves overcoming the mental hurdles that often follow individuals after incarceration. The impact of imprisonment can touch every facet of life, from career opportunities to the depth of personal relationships. It's like embarking on a fresh start while lugging around a heavy backpack filled with old burdens. Suppose we aspire to genuinely uplift those transitioning from prison. In that case, we must address these mental health challenges directly, delivering authentic, impactful support at every step.

The Path Forward: A Journey of Healing and Hope

Grasping the mental health repercussions of incarceration is essential for creating real, positive change. It goes beyond what transpires behind prison walls; it's about how we can foster healing for those who have endured such experiences. By promoting open conversations and providing heartfelt assistance, we can disrupt the cycle of trauma and give former inmates a genuine chance at a fresh beginning. Let's unite in this mission to guarantee that when individuals cross those prison gates, they enter not just a new world but a realm rich with opportunities for healing and hope.

Exploring the Parallels Between Prison Life and Modern Existence

In my poem, "Hard Knock Life," I vividly portray the stark realities of prison life challenging conditions, limited freedoms, and the daily struggle for survival. While this portrayal may seem intense, it intriguingly resonates with aspects of our modern existence when we consider our daily routines and societal structures. Let's delve into how these two worlds intertwine:

1. **Restricted Freedom and Illusions of Choice**

In prison, life is characterized by limitations and a rigid schedule, where personal autonomy is largely absent. Choices may be diminished to trivial matters in a highly controlled environment.

In modern life, we might not be physically confined, but many elements of contemporary living can feel similarly constraining. Advertising, social media trends, and the relentless search for convenience often influence our decisions. This illusion of choice can feel hollow amidst the pressures of digital notifications and societal expectations.

2. **Artificial Sustenance and Fulfilment of Needs**

My poem reflects on the appalling quality of prison food meagre, tasteless, and far from nourishing. This lack of adequate sustenance symbolizes a broader sense of deprivation felt during incarceration.

Likewise, while many food options surround us, many are processed and designed more for convenience than nutrition. This stark contrast between choices' appearance and quality is reminiscent of the artificial sustenance found in prisons.

3. **Isolation and Genuine Connection**

Isolation lies at the core of prison life, highlighting the physical and emotional separation from the outside world. My poem brings this feeling to life through vivid depictions of solitary confinement and the scarcity of social interaction.

In today's world, despite our digital connectivity, many people grapple with an escalating sense of emotional isolation. While online interactions are abundant, they often lack the depth of face-to-face connections, leaving individuals feeling lonely even amidst a sea of digital acquaintances. This similarity can intensify feelings of disconnection.

4. **Coping Mechanisms and Escaping Reality**

Inmates often resort to various coping strategies to navigate their harsh environments, from forming alliances to finding solace in routines. These mechanisms are vital for their mental resilience.

Similarly, we develop our coping mechanisms to manage the stresses of daily life—whether that means binge-watching TV shows or scrolling through social media. Just as prisoners find comfort in their routines, these choices provide a brief respite from the monotony and pressures of contemporary living.

5. **False Appearances and Deceptive Comforts**

The poem reveals the misleading nature of comfort within prison walls. Small luxuries like workout time or social games - starkly contrast the harsh conditions, offering only temporary relief from fundamental deprivations.

Likewise, the conveniences of modern life often mask deeper feelings of dissatisfaction. The allure of instant gratification from technology and consumerism can overshadow a more profound sense of self-fulfilment, reflecting a polished facade that can conceal underlying emptiness.

6. Survival and the Quest for Meaning

Survivors in prison must adeptly navigate complex social dynamics and personal challenges. My poem emphasizes the struggle to cultivate meaning and maintain a strong sense of identity within the constraints of incarceration.

In our modern world, we also face challenges from balancing work and personal life to seeking purpose. This search for meaning drives us not just to exist but to thrive.

We can foster an environment where healing and hope flourish by recognizing these parallels and embracing the importance of understanding and compassion. Let's join forces to pave the way for meaningful change, ensuring that everyone has the opportunity to embark on their journey toward a brighter future!

6

Fear, Mental Health, and Self-Hatred: Finding Balance in the Chaos

Focus:

This chapter delves into the profound influence of fear, often the unseen force behind self-doubt, anxiety, and the repetitive thought patterns that hold us back. It uncovers how fear embeds itself in our minds, shapes our surroundings, and masquerades as self-hatred, worry, and isolation. This is a powerful invitation to shift our perspective: instead of viewing fear as an adversary, we should embrace it as a messenger that leads us toward greater awareness, self-compassion, and intentional living. By recognizing fear in this way, we can reclaim our lives and unlock our true potential.

Transmissions From Earth Realm:

- *"Fear doesn't just lock the doors — it hands you the key and convinces you not to use it."*
- *"Most of what we call 'self-hate' is fear wearing a mask."*
- *"The mind can be a haunted house, echoing with threats that never materialize."*
- *"When you fear the unknown, you forget you were born to explore it."*
- *"Society doesn't sell safety — it sells fear, neatly packaged as protection."*
- *"Your environment isn't neutral; it either nourishes your spirit or feeds your fears."*
- *"Awakening starts when you stop letting fear think for you."*

> *"Terrible thing to live in fear. Brooks Hatlen knew it. Knew it all too well. All I want is to be back where things make sense. Where I won't have to be afraid all the time."*
> ***– Shawshank Redemption (1994)***

Did you know?

Understanding Fear's Grip on the Mind: Fear, with its overpowering nature, can hijack our brain's natural functions. The amygdala, the brain's fear centre, evaluates threats and can trigger extreme reactions, sometimes causing irrational behaviour and overwhelming anxiety. This understanding empowers us to take control of our responses and manage our fears. **The Perpetual Cycle**: Fear can perpetuate itself. Chronic fear responses can lead to heightened levels of cortisol and adrenaline, which, if sustained, contribute to long-term health problems such as heart disease and chronic anxiety disorders.

1. **Phobias and Development**: While many phobias begin in childhood or adolescence, they can become deeply ingrained and persist into adulthood. These phobias can severely limit a person's life, influencing their daily activities and relationships.
2. **Public Speaking Paralysis**: Glossophobia, or the fear of public speaking, affects around 75% of people. This fear can be debilitating, often leading individuals to avoid opportunities that require speaking in front of others, impacting their professional and personal lives.
3. **The Fear of the Unknown**: Up to 30% of people have arachnophobia, the fear of spiders. This intense fear can lead individuals to avoid certain places or situations, even if the threat is minimal or non-existent.

Why So Serious?

We all have fears that lurk in the corners of our minds, but many of us keep them hidden, afraid of what might happen if our vulnerabilities are exposed. Ironically, the fear of our fears being used against us often keeps us silent.

When I was younger, fear seemed like an all-encompassing fog. But as I grew older, faced challenges, and understood my own demons, those fears began to dissipate like mist in the morning sun. I strive to connect my emotions with logic, avoiding the trap of overthinking that can lead to a paralyzing spiral of anxiety.

So, what scares me? I fear being silenced or misrepresented

by deceitful narratives that don't reflect who I am. I worry about abandonment from those I care about and being judged through the lens of harmful stereotypes. The fear that people might view me as just another black male fitting negative stereotypes is a weight I carry. I worry about the lack of genuine individual thinking, which isn't influenced by media or hearsay. I fear the loss of friends and family to circumstances that I might not control, and the thought of dying with truths left unspoken haunts me. It feels like a race against time, where the door to opportunities might close before I've had a chance to make an impact. But I refuse to let that stop me; I'm determined to forge my path, even if it means creating opportunities.

Who am I trying to impress? In essence, it's the fear of being judged or, more accurately, of being misunderstood. I don't want to be just another statistic, another face in the crowd. The future can seem bleak, but I remind myself I'm here to make a difference. When you start to shine, it's as if dark forces take notice and try to snuff out your light. The game is dirty, and I've seen it firsthand. Sometimes, it feels like a blame game where hypocrisy thrives, and you're left feeling deflated, hoping for a breakthrough.

Facing our fears is arguably one of the hardest things we can do. But when confronting them, we reclaim our power and liberate ourselves from their oppressive hold. Ignoring them won't make them disappear; they'll only grow in power. As uncomfortable and terrifying as it may be, we must face our fears head-on, resolve them, and reclaim our power. Be the example that turns negativity into strength and sends that darkness back to where it came from.

What is Fear?

Understanding Fear: Fear is an emotion that arises in response to perceived threats or danger. It is a basic human instinct designed to protect us from harm. By understanding its triggers and responses, we can better prepare ourselves to manage and overcome our fears.

When fear strikes, our bodies enter "fight or flight" mode. This response triggers a series of physiological changes: increased heart rate, rapid breathing, sweating, muscle tension, and a surge of adrenaline. These reactions prepare us to confront or escape the threat. Alongside these physical changes, fear generates a torrent of thoughts and feelings of worry, anxiety, panic, dread, and terror. The amygdala, a crucial part of the brain's limbic system, plays a central role in fear responses. It evaluates threats and initiates the body's fear response, modifying neuron connections and activating the fight-or-flight mechanism.

Fear prompts various coping behaviours, from freezing and fleeing to fighting or hiding. Avoidance is also common, as is the response to seemingly benign stimuli perceived as threatening. Fear is deeply personal and subjective, shaped by individual experiences and perceptions. It can be triggered by various stimuli, from dangerous animals and heights to social judgment and the fear of failure.

Function of Fear

Fear isn't just an inconvenient guest at our mental dinner party; it's a built-in alarm system to keep us safe. It's like having a personal bodyguard who's always on high alert. When fear works as intended, it sharpens our senses and awareness. But when it oversteps its bounds, it can become a paralytic monster, robbing us of our joy and spontaneity. Think of fear as that annoying friend who tries to protect you from everything, even from having a good time.

Our brains are hardwired to fear. This evolutionary perk kept our ancestors alive by making them wary of threats like venomous snakes or ferocious predators. Today's fears of public speaking, heights, or spiders might not be as life-threatening, but they can still trip us up. Luckily, we have coping strategies like exposure therapy, cognitive-behavioural techniques, and support from others to help manage excessive fear. Embracing some fear is normal and even beneficial, as long as it doesn't turn into a full-blown anxiety apocalypse.

Dysfunctional Fear

Dysfunctional fear is like fear's evil twin: excessive, irrational, and stubborn. Imagine fearing dogs because of a childhood bite, even though most dogs today are harmless. Dysfunctional fear lingers long after the actual threat has disappeared, turning everyday situations into potential disaster zones. It can keep you from enjoying life, disrupt relationships, and even make you feel like a prisoner in your own mind.

Avoidance might seem like a quick fix, but it only reinforces the fear, making it harder to deal with in the long run. Instead of avoiding your fears, tackling them head-on is key. Dysfunctional fear can lead to obsessive behaviours and a diminished quality of life. Facing and addressing your fears is crucial to reclaiming your freedom and well-being.

Fear and Excitement

Fear and excitement are like twins separated at birth; one is the anxious introvert, and the other is the thrill-seeking extrovert. Both involve the same physiological responses: a racing heart, sweaty palms, and heightened focus. They're the body's way of gearing up for either battle or adventure.

Fear protects us from danger, while excitement drives us toward new experiences. While they might seem like opposites, they can mix in thrilling situations, like roller coasters or horror movies, where fear and excitement coalesce into thrilling rides. Reframing fear as a form of excitement can turn a nerve-wracking moment into an exhilarating opportunity.

90% of Phobias Occur During Childhood and Adolescence

Here's a fun fact: about 90% of phobias start in childhood or adolescence. It's like getting a fear starter pack at a young age. These early experiences shape our fear responses, making them feel almost hardwired. But don't worry, while childhood plays a significant role, it's not the end-all. Our fears can evolve with us. Genetics, temperament, and ongoing experiences contribute to our fear landscape, showing that while our early years are crucial, they're not the only chapter in our fear story.

Rising Above Fear with Compassion

Looking around today, it's hard not to notice the palpable sense of fear and anxiety that seems to hang in the air. People's low energy and sombre expressions reflect an inner struggle that feels all too familiar. Fear is a timeless companion, always lurking just out of sight. We face a choice: let fear consume us or respond with empathy, understanding, and wisdom.

Often, the roots of fear run deeper than personal worries. They're entwined with systemic issues that breed hopelessness and disconnection. It's not just about rising above our fears but also acknowledging the real psychological, physical, and economic pressures that affect us all.

Let's not meet fear with judgment but with compassion. By building genuine communities, listening to each other's stories, and promoting justice, we can help those overwhelmed by anxiety find their inner strength. With love and awareness, we can transform fear from a paralyzing force into a catalyst for positive change for ourselves and society.

Worry

Worry is like a mental hamster wheel, spinning endlessly as we obsess over hypothetical disasters that may never happen. Our mind attempts to control the uncontrollable, draining the present moment of its potential. The more we worry, the more exhausted and anxious we become, tackling the challenges we fret about even harder.

Instead of letting worry sap our strength, we need to anchor ourselves in the present. Focus on what we can influence now rather than getting lost in hypothetical catastrophes. In the here and now, fear has much less power than our resilient human spirit.

I used to worry deeply about people and their struggles. Friends would say, "Worrying is pointless." Still, I found that worry, when approached thoughtfully, can be more than just idle rumination. It signifies that we care and want to understand and solve problems. Instead of dismissing worry, we can explore its roots and share our concerns with trusted friends. Those heart-to-heart conversations provide valuable insights and ease our minds.

Worry isn't the core issue; it's a symptom of deeper fears and desires for connection. When approached openly, it can lead to meaningful self-discoveries and foster understanding. But worry alone won't solve problems. By turning our worries into actionable insights and trying to address them, we can transform unease into meaningful action. Our worries, when understood, connect us to what truly matters.

Conscious Awareness

We're multidimensional spiritual beings having a human experience, but let's face it, modern life often feels like a cosmic joke. We're running around chasing material gain, conformity, and status while our deeper selves are waving frantically from the sidelines. The disconnect from nature, each other, and our true selves is authentic, not just a mid-life crisis.

Societal norms often feel like a bad reality show, pushing us to conform and obey. But here's the kicker: we've got an inner power just waiting for us to tap into it. By practising conscious awareness, we can reconnect with our core essence and purpose and extend that compassion to others struggling with the same existential hangover.

It's not about dividing ourselves into "us vs. them" but coming together to tackle oppression and build a society where everyone can think freely and love unconditionally. Progress starts from within, and if we embrace our shared humanity while nurturing our divine nature, we can transform fear into freedom and create a world where spiritual enlightenment is the norm, not the exception.

Collective Consciousness Response

So, there's a buzz about "awakening" our consciousness to see beyond societal conditioning and tap into higher wisdom. Meditation, introspection, and the mysterious "decalcifying" of the pineal gland are all the rage. But let's be real, not everyone's ready for this spiritual buffet.

We can't force our awakening recipes onto others; think of it as trying to get a horse to drink water. Pushing too hard makes people dig in their heels. But some folks are already on their awakening journey, navigating through the psychological and social muck to elevate collective consciousness.

Awakening isn't a straight path or a quick fix; it's like a rollercoaster with unexpected loops. But with patience, compassion, and a sprinkle of support, we can help spread the seeds of greater awareness. We aim to infuse more love, justice, and fulfilment into our human experience. By shining our light, we can guide others when they're ready, and together, we can manifest humanity's spiritual destiny.

Fear's Grip

Fear is often used as a tool of control to keep us in line and make us surrender our power. It's like having a personal trainer who specializes in making you anxious. External sources of fear can manipulate us into conforming and feeling powerless. But fear also has a sneaky way of creeping into our minds, creating imaginary threats that trap us in a cycle of isolation and self-doubt.

Here's the good news: fear doesn't have to be our constant companion. We can break free from its grip through mindful awareness, critical reflection, and connecting with our intuition. By taking charge of our thoughts, we can respond thoughtfully rather than react in fear.

Our true nature is compassion, and by recognizing how we've projected our insecurities onto situations, we realize we're not at the mercy of external forces. Instead, we're the masters of our inner state. Shining a light on our fears helps us transcend them, moving beyond a culture of polite silence to one of open, thoughtful dialogue.

Yes, questioning deeply held beliefs and societal narratives can be uncomfortable, but that's where growth happens. We can't let the fear of offending others or facing discomfort stop us from speaking our truths and expanding our understanding. Embracing diverse views and fostering honest dialogue pushes us all towards essential truths. So, let's step out of our comfort zones and embark on this journey of awakening with courage, openness, and care.

Why is Mental Health Met with So Much Misunderstanding and Fear?

Mental health often gets a bad rap, like that one party guest who shows up uninvited and never seems to leave. Imagine mental health issues as the mysterious, shadowy corners of our psyche, places where the light doesn't always reach and where misconceptions can easily fester.

First off, there's a knowledge gap. Mental health can seem as alien as a language we've never heard before. If we're not educated about it, it feels like trying to understand quantum physics after a coffee. Fear often accompanies the unknown, and when mental health issues don't fit into our neat, tidy categories, they become fodder for myths and wild guesses.

Then there's the stigma, the stubborn cloud that hovers over mental health like a bad smell. This stigma, fuelled by outdated stereotypes and ignorance, often leads people to label those struggling as weak, lazy, or just plain unstable. It's like the easy way out: judge and label rather than deal with the messiness of genuine understanding.

Fear plays a significant role, too. Mental health issues can make us confront our own vulnerabilities and the precarious nature of our emotional well-being. It's like discovering your supposedly indestructible fortress has a few cracks. Still, it's unsettling to realize that our minds, which we often think of as solid and reliable, can be so easily shaken.

Lastly, the silence surrounding mental health doesn't help. When conversations about mental well-being are hushed or stigmatized, we're left in the dark, festering in ignorance. It's like trying to solve a puzzle without all the pieces: we just reinforce myths and feed our fears.

So, what's the fix? We must shed light on those shadowy corners by educating ourselves and engaging in open, honest conversations. We can build a more compassionate and informed approach to mental health by facing our fears head-on and challenging misconceptions. Let's turn down the volume on stigma and tune into understanding and empathy.

Fear and Environment: The Impact of Our Surroundings on Mental Health

Our environment profoundly influences our mental well-being, shaping the fears we face and how we navigate them. Imagine a vibrant cityscape where the hum of life is incessant. Still, underneath the surface, a different kind of noise thrives—a noise born of stress, anxiety, and fear. This backdrop can be more than just a setting; it can become a breeding ground for self-doubt and self-hatred.

When we talk about a toxic environment, we're referring to physical spaces and the social and emotional climates that permeate our lives. The places where we spend our time, the people we interact with, and the societal pressures we encounter all contribute to the internal chaos we experience.

Fear is often a product of our environment. For example, living in a neighbourhood plagued by crime can instil a pervasive sense of danger, leading to heightened anxiety and a constant state of alertness. This continuous stress doesn't just affect our immediate feelings of fear but also seeps into our mental health, causing long-term damage. We begin to internalize these fears, which can lead to self-hatred—believing we are powerless or flawed because we can't escape these conditions.

Moreover, environments characterized by high levels of negativity and toxicity can exacerbate feelings of inadequacy and self-loathing. When surrounded by pessimism, judgment, or harsh criticism, it's easy to start doubting our self-worth. Constant exposure to such environments can distort our self-image, making us feel trapped in a cycle of self-hatred, where we blame ourselves for not thriving despite these challenges.

Yet, it's crucial to recognize that our environment doesn't solely define us. We can reshape our mental landscape by changing our surroundings or altering our responses to them. Awareness is the first step in acknowledging how our environment impacts our mental health, which allows us to take proactive steps towards change. This might involve seeking supportive relationships, creating positive spaces, or setting boundaries to protect our mental well-being.

The journey to overcoming fear and self-hatred within a toxic environment is not about pretending these issues don't exist. Instead, it's about confronting them with courage and finding ways to reclaim our power. By fostering environments that nurture rather than deplete, we can start to heal and build a stronger, healthier self.

Understanding the connection between fear and the environment empowers us to take control of our mental health and break free from the patterns of self-destruction. It's about creating a safe space within ourselves and our surroundings to confront our fears and mend the wounds inflicted by a toxic environment.

Fear and Self-Hatred: The Connection

Fear and self-hatred are deeply intertwined, often feeding off each other in a vicious cycle. At its core, self-hatred can be seen as a manifestation of internal fear. When we hate ourselves, we're usually afraid of not measuring up, being unworthy, or failing to meet our or others' expectations. This internal fear morphs into self-loathing as we internalize these fears and project them onto ourselves.

In many ways, self-hatred is fear turned inward. It's the result of a deep-seated fear of inadequacy or failure. When we're afraid of not being good enough or falling short, that fear can erode our self-esteem, leading to self-criticism and, ultimately, self-hatred. The more we berate ourselves, the more entrenched our fears become, creating a feedback loop where fear fuels self-hatred, and self-hatred exacerbates our worries.

It's a harsh statement, but there's some truth to the idea that all hate derives from self-hate. Hate directed towards others often stems from unresolved self-hatred. When we can't confront our own flaws or insecurities, we might project our self-loathing onto others, using them as a scapegoat for the negative feelings we harbour about ourselves. This projection can manifest as anger, resentment, or outright hatred towards others, serving as a defence mechanism to shield ourselves from facing our internal turmoil.

Understanding this connection can be a key step in addressing self-hatred and the broader spectrum of negative emotions it can produce. By addressing our internal fears and fostering self-compassion, we can break the cycle of self-hatred and reduce the need to project our internal struggles onto others.

Turning Fear into Enlightenment

When we take the time to explore the roots of our fears, we begin to see their power for what really is an illusion. Imagine fears as shadows in a dark room; the more we shed light on them through knowledge and experience, the smaller and less intimidating they become. By confronting our fears, we can transform the unsettling sensations of dread into sparks of excitement and confidence.

Fear frees us in place, like a storm that makes us hesitate to step outside. Yet, excitement and curiosity are like the sun breaking through the clouds, urging us to venture out and embrace the unknown. Courage involves learning when to push past those fears and beliefs that confine us, allowing us to take risks and grow.

However, achieving true enlightenment involves more than just overcoming our personal fears. Once we've navigated our shadows, we can help others still in darkness. Ultimately, we are not waiting for someone to rescue us; we must become heroes.

Our collective enlightenment won't come from external prophets or grand revelations. Instead, it will emerge from the inner light that shines within us. Think of ourselves as beacons, lighting up our path and guiding others through their fog of fear. We must regain control of our journey, steering our course with intention and clarity.

When we awaken from the illusions of fear, we pave the way for a society driven by purpose and inspiration rather than anxiety. Suppose we recognize and ignite the light within all of humanity. In that case, we can look forward to a future that is not just brighter but truly transformative.

Key Points:

- **Recognize and Rewrite Fear:** Fear often results from ingrained societal and childhood programming. We must actively challenge and change these limiting beliefs to move past fear by controlling our influences and environment.
- **Seek Growth Through Positivity:** Although external circumstances can hinder growth, we have the power to broaden our perspectives by seeking truth, engaging in self-work, and surrounding ourselves with positive influences.
- **Inner Transformation First:** True happiness and freedom come from within. Instead of seeking external validation or assigning blame, focus on personal responsibility and align with your purpose to unleash your full potential.
- **Lead by Example:** After achieving personal enlightenment, extend support to others by sharing your insights and experiences. Remember, Transformation is individual, and we can only offer guidance, not force change.
- **Confront and Transcend Fear:** To evolve collectively, we must examine and question our programmed fears and false beliefs. By reclaiming control over our minds, we shift from reactive fear to empowered, conscious creation.

Key Actions:

- Engage in self-work to reprogram limiting beliefs.
- Lead by example with humility and compassion.

- Understand and challenge fear as an illusion.
- Embrace personal responsibility and alignment with your highest self.

7

Chasing Shadows: The Many Faces of Addiction

Focus:

This chapter explores addiction's haunting landscape, revealing its chemical, emotional, and behavioural facets while addressing the underlying pain shaping them. It encourages us to look beyond stigma and labels to uncover unmet needs, unhealed wounds, and a deep longing for connection. Through compassionate curiosity, we can dismantle myths about addiction and reclaim the silenced parts of ourselves. It's time to confront the truth and reclaim our narratives.

Transmissions From Earth Realm:

- *"We don't seek the high for pleasure; we seek it for relief."*
- *"Addiction isn't a choice, it's the echo of a wound still waiting to be heard."*
- *"What we call addiction is often just self-soothing, practised*

in the shadows, when no one else was listening."

- *"You aren't weak for falling into the trap, you were surviving the only way you knew how."*
- *"Substances don't enslave us, it's the unresolved pain beneath them that tightens the chains."*
- *"Recovery doesn't begin when you quit; it begins when you finally stop running from yourself."*

Did you know?

1. **Addiction significantly alters the brain's reward system.** Substances or behaviours hijack the brain's natural pleasure pathways, making it extremely challenging to stop despite harmful consequences. This results in lasting changes to behaviour and mental health.
2. **Genetics account for up to 60% of addiction vulnerability.** If addiction is prevalent in your family, your risk of developing an addiction is higher due to genetic predispositions.
3. **Nicotine addiction has one of the lowest lifetime recovery rates.** Less than 10% of individuals who attempt to quit smoking manage to stay smoke-free long-term, demonstrating the deeply entrenched nature of nicotine dependence.
4. **Trauma and mental health disorders are closely linked to higher addiction risks.** Conditions like PTSD, anxiety, and depression often lead individuals to use substances as a form of self-medication.

5. **Behavioural addictions can be as destructive as substance addictions.** Gambling, gaming, and social media can have similarly severe impacts on individuals' lives, mental health, and overall well-being.

> *"Addiction denied is recovery delayed."* - ***Mokokoma Mokhonoana.***

Understanding the Beast - Defining Addiction

Addiction isn't just a stubborn habit or a lack of self-discipline; it's a chronic, relapsing disorder that disrupts your brain's reward system, stress response, and self-control mechanisms. Imagine your brain as a high-tech gadget that's been hacked. Addiction rewires your internal circuits, making you hit 'retry' on your vices no matter how much havoc it wreaks.

In essence, addiction is like a software glitch that affects your brain's reward, stress, and self-control circuits. It's not just about the visible fallout but the deep-rooted changes affecting your entire system. This isn't a matter of willpower alone; it's a complex interplay of genetic, developmental, and environmental factors like a recipe where genetics, life experiences, and surroundings blend to create a unique, often troubling dish.

When you throw mental illness and trauma into the mix, it's like adding extra spice to an already intense recipe. The combination creates a tangled mess that's difficult to unravel, making addiction a frequent companion to mental health struggles and past traumas.

As Mokokoma Mokhonoana wisely said, "Addiction denied is recovery delayed." Acknowledging addiction isn't just about recognizing a problem. It's about confronting the core issues to start the journey toward healing. Like admitting that your favourite app has a bug, facing addiction requires understanding, compassion, and a commitment to fixing what's broken.

"First, you take a drink, then the drink takes a drink, then the drink takes you." – **F. Scott Fitzgerald**.

Let's face it: we're all addicts in some form or another. Whether it's caffeine, social media likes, or that toxic relationship you swear you'll leave tomorrow, we all have our vices. But admitting you have an addiction? That's the real struggle. It's easier to stay in denial, rolling your eyes at anyone brave enough to point out the obvious. But you're not alone in this. Many of us are on this journey with you.

Addiction is a merciless thief, robbing you of your relationships, job prospects, and even your sanity. It's the ultimate life-wrecker, causing mental breakdowns and health problems that feel like they're impossible to undo. And if you let it run its course, you might as well kiss your future goodbye.

Speaking from experience, I've had my fair share of vices. Luckily, I never went full throttle on the self-destruction train, but I've been close enough to the tracks to know how easy it is to get derailed. There was a time when I wouldn't have touched drugs or alcohol with a ten-foot pole, but life has a funny way of changing your mind. It started innocently enough with doctor-prescribed antidepressants as a teen. Before I knew it, I was more open to experimenting.

Sure, I've dabbled. I tried marijuana and played around with more complicated stuff just to see what all the fuss was about. And you know what? It was a colossal waste of time and money. But not everyone's as stubborn as I am. I've seen people get sucked into the vortex of addiction, held hostage by their cravings, and buried under drug debts that never seem to go away.

When you're in deep, you've got to ask yourself, "Am I in control, or is this shit controlling me?" Once you've got your answer, it's time to fight back. Because trust me, the longer you wait, the harder it gets.

But let's get one thing straight: nobody should be demonized for their addictions. Most of the time, it's just a phase and a little support from a solid circle of friends can make all the difference. When you're talking to someone struggling, start with the positives. Remind them of who they really are before diving into what they risk.

To the addicts out there, yeah, I'm talking to you, get your shit together. The people who love you have every right to cut you off if you're not bringing anything good to the table. They don't have to accept what you've become. But remember those drugs? They're not you, so don't get it twisted. The best version of yourself is waiting, and it's on you to break free from the chains of addiction. Recovery is possible, and the first step is believing in yourself.

You're the key to your own freedom. You've got the power to turn it all around with commitment, courage, and discipline. And remember, you don't have to do it alone. There's support out there, and you just need to find the right fit. You're not alone in this journey, and some people care about you and want to see you succeed.

There is no doubt in my mind that we have all been there

before or are still presently dealing with some form or degree of addiction. It can be challenging to admit we have an addiction, leaving us in denial on the defensive when somebody calls it out.

Addiction can and will destroy lives and relationships, employment prospects and social interactions. Addiction is at the core of many mental breakdowns and physical health problems. If unresolved, the costly consequences and effects can appear to be irreversible.

What are the Key Factors of Addiction?

So, you think your addiction is all about willpower? Guess again. Genetics has a big hand in whether you will end up hooked. If addiction runs in your family, you might as well consider yourself pre-approved. Twin studies suggest that your genes account for about 40-60% of your addiction risk. In other words, you might be wired for self-destruction before starting.

The brain's reward system, which makes you feel good when you do something pleasurable, can be a bit of a backstabber. If your brain's wiring is faulty, you might not get enough natural highs, pushing you to seek out artificial ones. Specific genetic quirks can make your brain respond to dopamine like a dog chasing its tail round and round you go, with no end in sight.

In short, if Uncle Joe couldn't put down the bottle, you might want to watch your habits. Your brain could be set up to make that first drink or hit feel like the best decision ever right up until it isn't.

Early Use

Think starting young doesn't matter? Think again. If you're hitting the bottle or lighting up before figuring out algebra, you're setting yourself up for a long, rough ride. The adolescent brain is still under construction, especially the part that handles decision-making and impulse control. Teens are hardwired for risk-taking and thrill-seeking, which makes that first hit of dopamine from drugs or alcohol feel like a jackpot.

But here's the catch: while you're chasing that high, your brain's wiring is getting rerouted, not in a good way. The pathways that reinforce addiction get stronger, making it harder to break the cycle later on. If you start drinking before you can legally drive, your chances of becoming an alcoholic quadruple.

Starting with nicotine, booze, or weed in your early teens? You might as well be laying the foundation for a lifelong battle with addiction. So, think twice the next time someone offers you a drink at 14. Your future self will thank you.

The Serious Comedy of Addiction and Mental Health

Ever wondered why your brain feels like it's running Windows 95 while everyone else seems to be on the latest Mac? That's what mental health disorders like depression, anxiety, PTSD, and ADHD do. They mess with your brain's wiring, making you hit 'Ctrl+Alt+Delete' on your emotions. To cope, some folks turn to self-medication. After all, who needs therapy when you've got a bottle of 'feel-better-now'?

But here's the kicker: what starts as a quick fix can become a vicious cycle. Drugs and alcohol might offer a temporary escape. Still, they're also expert saboteurs, quietly making things worse while pretending to be your friend. It's like hiring a raccoon as your life coach. Sure, it's entertaining initially, but soon enough, everything's in shambles, and you're knee-deep in the trash.

Environment: The Stress Cooker

Picture this: you're stuck in a pressure cooker with no off switch. High stress, low income, and a lack of support turn life into a game of 'How much can you handle before you crack?' And when everything around you is burning, sometimes reaching for that cold beer or hitting that joint feels the only way to cool off.

But if you're surrounded by people who think popping pills is as normal as popping gum, it's easy to fall into the same habits. And let's be real: peer pressure isn't just for teenagers; it's like a contagious yawn with much worse consequences.

Trauma: The Uninvited Guest

Trauma is when one guest shows up unannounced, wrecks your place, and overstays their welcome. Childhood trauma, in particular, leaves a lasting impact, messing with your brain's emotional controls like a bad DJ at a party. And when life's playlist is nothing but bad memories on repeat, some turn to substances for a change of tune.

But drugs and alcohol are terrible therapists—they promise relief but end up charging you in health, happiness, and hope. It's a trap that's hard to escape, like quicksand in an emotional desert.

Compulsive Tendencies: The Urge to Splurge

Ever have that urge to binge-watch a whole season in one night? Now, imagine that urge, but instead of Netflix, it's drugs or alcohol. Impulsive and compulsive behaviours are like that annoying itch you can't help but scratch, even though you know it's just making things worse. For some, this itch drives them straight into addiction, where they get stuck on repeat, chasing a high that's always just out of reach.

The Ripple Effect: Addiction's Impact

Addiction isn't just a personal problem; it's like tossing a boulder into a pond—the ripples hit everyone around you. Your health takes a nosedive, relationships crumble under the weight of lies and broken promises, and soon enough, your job and finances are circling the drain. It's like being the star of your own disaster movie, except there's no heroic rescue at the end.

And let's not forget the societal costs. From healthcare to criminal justice, addiction drains resources faster than you can say, "Where did all the money go?" But there's hope prevention and rehabilitation can flip the script, turning that tragic story into redemption.

In the end, addiction is no laughing matter, but sometimes, finding humour in the darkness helps us see the light. After all, if we can laugh about it, we can do something about it too.

Health: The Body's Overdue Repair Bill

Addiction treats your body like a demolition derby vehicle, except you're not winning any trophies. From liver damage to lung issues, your organs are getting a front-row seat to the chaos. It's like giving your body a VIP pass to the worst party ever, where the drinks are laced with toxins and the music never stops.

Your mental health isn't spared either. Addiction and mental illness make a perfect storm, creating cognitive deficits and mood swings that could give a soap opera a run for its money. It's not just about feeling lousy; it's about turning your well-being into a full-time project that even the best doctors struggle to fix.

Relationships: The Trust Erosion Express

Addiction is the ultimate relationship wrecking ball. Picture this: every lie, broken promise, and erratic behaviour is like adding another layer of grime to your friendships and family ties. Trust gets shredded faster than a discount store's holiday sale, leaving nothing but emotional debris.

As the addiction takes centre stage, everyone else gets relegated to the sidelines. It's a tragic play where loved ones get caught in the crossfire of your substance-fuelled drama. Friendships may dissolve, and families might disintegrate, leaving you isolated in a pit of your own making.

Education: Failing Grades and Empty Desks

Addiction turns school and work into an afterthought, like a bad sequel that nobody asked for. The focus shifts from learning and growth to securing the next high, leading to missed classes and spotty performance. It's like running on a treadmill that's constantly speeding up. You're always out of breath and never getting anywhere.

For those in the workforce, addiction means missed deadlines, accidents, and performance dips. Your career path becomes a series of wrong turns, leading straight to unemployment and a tarnished resume. The skills you've honed get rusty, and job prospects vanish faster than a paycheck on payday.

Finances: The Wallet Black Hole

Addiction has a built-in feature: it turns your bank account into a black hole. Every dollar you earn seems to disappear into the void of your next fix. It's a financial vortex where bills, rent, and savings go up in smoke, leaving only a pile of debt and a desperate scramble for cash.

Medical bills, legal fees, and treatment costs add insult to injury, turning your financial situation into a cautionary tale. Your assets evaporate, and you're left trying to explain to creditors why you're broke despite the fact you've been working full-time.

Crime: The Desperate Side Hustle

When addiction meets desperation, crime often makes an appearance. Picture it: you're in a tight spot, so why not boost a few wallets or break into a store? Theft, violence, and drug dealing become everyday business, turning your life into a crime spree montage.

The addiction-fueled crime wave doesn't just affect you; it spills over into your community, ramping up crime rates and straining law enforcement resources. The cycle of crime and punishment becomes a grim reality, making you a permanent fixture in the local news cycle.

The Bottom Line

Addiction is a relentless thief that robs your health, relationships, education, finances, and freedom. But there's a twist in this dark comedy: with the right help and a solid recovery plan, you can rewrite the script and reclaim your life. It's not just about surviving the fallout. It's about fighting back and turning the page on your personal tragedy.

The Stigma Trap: Why Addicts Get the Short End of the Stick

Addiction's got a bad reputation, and it's not just from being the life of the trashy reality TV show. The stigma attached to addiction is like having a giant "Do Not Enter" sign on the road to recovery. It's that extra layer of judgment that makes people feel like they're not just battling their addiction but also fighting an army of disapproving stares and condescending whispers.

When society treats addiction like a moral failing rather than a disease, it's like blaming someone for getting sick with the flu and then telling them to "just get over it." Addiction is not a character flaw or a personal failing. It's a disease that hijacks your brain, making it more challenging than ever to hit the brakes. It's like being locked in a room with an overzealous squirrel that keeps throwing nuts at you, whether you want them or not.

Compassion Over Condemnation: The Better Way Forward

To really tackle addiction, we need to kick stigma to the curb and recognize addiction as a disease, not a moral pitfall. Think of it like this: if we treated cancer patients the way we treat people with addiction, we'd be telling them they're just lazy and should try harder to "not be sick." Instead, we should focus on understanding the root causes like trauma, mental illness, and social isolation.

Compassion is key here. Imagine if we called them clumsy and ignored their pain every time someone stubbed their toe. That's precisely what happens when we shame people with addiction instead of supporting them. They don't need judgment; they need help, like how you'd help a friend locked out of their car rather than just making fun of their misfortune.

Stories and Empathy: The Secret Weapons in the Fight

Putting a human face on addiction helps break down the barriers of stigma. Support groups where people share their real experiences are like opening a window in a stuffy room. They let in fresh air and show there's more to a person than just their addiction. These stories remind us that behind every addiction is a person with dreams, struggles, and a whole lot of humanity.

Addicts deserve respect, love, and a shot at recovery. It's not about locking them up or shaming them into change. It's about offering them a path to get back on their feet because treating them like they're less than human does nothing but deepen the hole they're already in.

The Path Forward: A Call for Compassion

To truly address addiction, we need to make it visible, redefine it with compassion, and support it with understanding. Criminalizing addiction and locking people up just adds more weight to their already heavy burden. Instead, we should focus on scientifically guided treatments, public support, and a little empathy to make recovery possible.

So, let's flip the script on addiction and stigma. After all, if we can laugh about the absurdity of the situation, maybe we can turn that laughter into a powerful tool for change. Let's show people with addiction that they're not alone, they're not broken, and they certainly don't deserve to be treated like they're on the wrong side of a joke.

"You must break down before you can breakthrough." – Marilyn Ferguson.

Recovery: Breaking Down to Break Through

Ever heard the saying, "You have to break down before you can break through"? It's a reminder that sometimes life throws us into a tough spot before we can make real progress. When it comes to addiction, recovery is absolutely possible, but it's not always a straightforward path. It's a challenging journey with ups and downs rather than a quick fix.

Addiction is often seen as a chronic, relapsing condition. Think of it as a long-term health issue and constant attention is needed. Some people hold onto the hope of complete recovery, while others view it as a lifelong battle. Success rates can vary widely. For instance, about 50-70% of alcoholics stay sober for the first year, but relapse rates over time can be pretty high. Nicotine addiction is even tougher, with lifetime recovery rates under 10%.

The Secret Sauce: What Makes Recovery Stick?

Maintaining recovery involves a combination of strategies and support. It's like keeping a plant healthy, with consistent care, avoiding harmful conditions, and sometimes giving it extra attention. Essential tools include support groups, therapy, medication, and learning to manage triggers. Recovery is a journey with ups and downs; occasional lapses don't mean failure. Resilience and a strong support network are key to staying on track.

Prevention and Interventions: A Playbook for Teens

For teens, it's essential to focus on prevention. Delaying the start of substance use, making drugs more challenging to access, and offering engaging, drug-free activities are crucial steps. Tailoring addiction education to their developmental stage can help steer them away from risky behaviours.

Evidence-based approaches are essential to keeping them safe and informed.

Integrated Treatment: The Dynamic Duo

When dealing with both addiction and mental health issues, addressing them together is most effective. Integrated treatment helps manage both conditions simultaneously. Building healthy coping strategies and receiving proper support can make a big difference in recovery.

The Societal Shift: From Glorification to Mindfulness

We also need to change how we view and talk about substance use. Instead of glorifying it, we should promote healthy living and fun without substances. Creating communities where engaging, drug-free activities are celebrated can help shift the focus. You can have a great time and enjoy life without relying on drugs or alcohol. Being mindful and present can elevate your experiences and help build a supportive environment.

In the end, recovery is a journey worth taking. With the proper support and approach, navigating the challenges and making lasting, positive changes are possible. It's about finding strength in the struggle and moving forward with hope and determination.

Final Thoughts: The Power of Compassion and Collective Responsibility

Addiction isn't just about drugs and alcohol. It's anything that distracts us from reality: gaming, social media, eating, you name it. This escapism isn't just about avoiding boredom; it's a complete detour from dealing with life's messiness. We end up trading our profound, fulfilling moments for fleeting highs that ultimately leave us stuck in a loop of self-defeat.

Now, let's get real: if we want a better society, we can't just ignore those struggling with addiction. Ostracizing them, stigmatizing them, or criminalizing them over issues that often start from deep-rooted mental health problems and harsh environments isn't helping. If we've failed them in the past, it's on us to pick up the slack now. Remember, it takes a village to raise a child. Where were we when these issues first began?

Instead of just pointing fingers, let's step up and address these issues together. We tend to sweep problems under the rug while getting caught up in our lives. The government might not be hitting the mark on addiction treatment, but that doesn't mean we're powerless. We can't just depend on underfunded systems that seem to have cash for wars but not for people's well-being. We must step in with our plans, resources, and collective power.

While it's true that not everyone can be helped, especially those deeply entrenched in their struggles, we can make a real difference by focusing on the younger generation. Let's break the cycle by sharing our experiences, spreading awareness, and steering them toward healthier lifestyles. They need to see the harsh realities not just through a critical lens but with a compassionate one.

So, will we keep clinging to the "survival of the fittest" mindset, or can we aim for "survival of a collaborative humanity"? Let's embrace the latter and make a collective effort to support, understand, and uplift those struggling with addiction. After all, a truly thriving society does not just leave people behind but actively works to bring everyone along.

Key Takeaways

1. **Understand Addiction as a Brain Disease:**Recognize that addiction is a complex condition affecting brain function, not just a personal choice or flaw.
2. **Identify and Address Risk Factors:**Be aware of significant risk factors like family history, mental health issues, early substance use, trauma, and impulsivity. Build protective factors such as strong support systems to mitigate these risks.
3. **Acknowledge the Impact of Addictive Substances:** Understand how substances hijack the brain's reward system, leading to compulsive behaviours. Recognize that behavioural addictions (like gambling) operate similarly.
4. **Combat Stigma:** Work to reduce stigma around addiction by promoting understanding and compassion, making it easier for people to seek help and support.
5. **Support Recovery Efforts:** Provide accessible treatment options and encourage lifestyle changes that aid recovery. Emphasize the importance of ongoing management and vigilance to prevent relapses.
6. **Focus on Prevention:** Implement strategies to prevent substance use in young people, limit access to harmful substances, and promote addiction education and support.
7. **Promote Compassionate Policies:** Advocate for policies that address the root causes of addiction, offer compassionate support, and employ evidence-based approaches to manage addiction as a societal issue.

8

Media Spin and Stigma: Who Are the Real Villains?

Focus:

This chapter confronts the manipulative web of media narratives and the viral nature of stigma, exposing how perception is shaped by words and who holds the microphone. It dives into how labels, stereotypes, and systemic bias are weaponized to maintain control, create division, and suppress truth. By unmasking the myths we've inherited, we reclaim our ability to think critically, live authentically, and stand in solidarity with the marginalized. It's time to debug the fear-based programming and rewrite the story. Together.

Transmissions From Earth Realm:

- *"Stigma is the scar society leaves on the soul, not the skin."*
- *"They don't just feed us lies. They starve us of truth."*
- *"When media builds the villain, ask who profits from the fear."*

- *"Your worth was never meant to fit inside their checkbox."*
- *"Stigma isn't born in truth. It's bred in ignorance, nurtured by silence."*
- *"The revolution begins when we question the narrative, not the person."*
- *"You are not the names they gave you. You are the truth they feared."*
- *"Freedom isn't just physical. It's mental, emotional, and spiritual."*
- *"They can't program a soul that chooses to awaken."*

Did You Know?

- **The Origin of Stigma**: The term "stigma" comes from ancient Greek, which meant a mark burned into the skin of slaves or criminals. Think of it as the original "label," but way more permanent and painful.
- **The Domino Effect of Stigma**: Ever notice how one stereotype can lead to another? For example, suppose someone is stigmatized for being overweight. In that case, they might also face prejudice if they have health conditions like diabetes. It's like one bad reputation snowballing into a whole avalanche.
- **Stereotype Threat**: This is when the fear of confirming a stereotype makes it come true. For instance, Black students might perform worse on tests if they're worried about living up to racial stereotypes. It's like a self-fulfilling prophecy meets academic pressure.

- **The "Why Bother?" Effect**: Self-stigma can make people wonder, "Why should I try?" If society keeps sending the message that they're not good enough, it's easy to give up before you even start.
- **Counteracting Stigma**: Want to help reduce Stigma? Positive representations in media can make a big difference. When people with mental health issues are shown in a positive light, it can help change attitudes and break down stereotypes.
- **Social Exclusion**: Stigma often means being shut out from important stuff like jobs, education, and healthcare. It's like being on the outside looking in while others get all the opportunities.
- **Discrimination in Disguise**: Stigma doesn't just hurt feelings. It can lead to real-world problems like losing job opportunities, struggling in school, or getting proper healthcare. It's a serious issue with tangible effects.

> *"If you're not careful, the newspapers will have you hating the people who are being oppressed and loving the people who are doing the oppressing."* —***Malcolm X***

Media Manipulation and the Power of Perception

"If you're not careful, the newspapers will have you hating the people who are being oppressed and loving the people who are doing the oppressing," said Malcolm X. And he wasn't kidding. Media is like a magician with a dark sense of humour, making you root for the villains and boo the heroes. This manipulation of perception has a profound impact on society, shaping our attitudes and beliefs. They've mastered spinning stories, choosing headlines, and painting the world in whatever shade suits their narrative. One minute, you're sympathizing with the oppressed and the next, you're convinced they're the real troublemakers. Meanwhile, the actual bad guys are getting standing ovations.

The Stigma Game: Labels and Power

So, what's the takeaway? Don't be a sucker. Don't gulp down the media's version of reality without a second thought. Instead, channel your inner detective, question everything, spot the biases (look for one-sided reporting, sensationalism, or lack of diverse perspectives), and don't let them mess with your head. Malcolm's words aren't just a warning. They're a challenge to think for yourself and stand with those who need it. After all, it's way cooler to be informed than to be a puppet on their string.

Stigma, meanwhile, is a complex beast that blends psychological and social dimensions with real-world consequences. It's essentially a cocktail of negative stereotypes, prejudices, and discriminatory behaviours swirling around a particular trait or identity. At its core, Stigma thrives on a power imbalance where specific individuals or groups get the social equivalent of a "Kick Me" sign simply because their characteristics are deemed undesirable.

Labels are the sneaky little tags society slaps on people based on race, gender, sexuality, mental health, physical abilities, or socioeconomic status. It's like playing a game of "Who Can Judge the Harshest," where those in power decide who's "in" and who's "out."

Stigmatization happens when this game combines stereotyping, separation, and all-around discrimination, letting the dominant crowd keep their thumbs firmly pressed down on marginalized groups.

Stigma is born from ignorance and fear, like being scared of clowns because of a bad birthday party experience. The consequences are no joke: diminished self-worth, psychological threats, and blocked opportunities, all adding up to a life on the sidelines. It's a social phenomenon that keeps inequality in business by upholding negative attitudes and robbing human diversity of its power.

Breaking the Cycle: Challenging Labels and Stigma

But here's the silver lining: Stigma isn't set in stone. It's a social construct, meaning it's as changeable as a wardrobe trend. With some education, empowerment, and a good dose of empathy, we can start swapping outdated biases for something more humanizing. Empathy, in particular, is a powerful tool in this fight, as it allows us to see beyond the labels and connect with the person underneath. Because, in the end, everyone deserves a spot at the table no matter what label society tries to stick on them.

From the moment we enter this world, society tries to put us into boxes. As soon as we're old enough to fill out forms, we're asked to check off our race, disabilities, and more. "It's just for data," they say. "To make sure everyone is treated fairly." Maybe so, but it often feels like that data gets used against us to limit opportunities or judge us before knowing our character. Well, I'm done with boxes. In the following form, I may just check "human being" and leave the rest blank. Who I am is so much more than any label could capture. What matters is the content of my character, not the colour of my skin or other factors out of my control. The categories never reasonably fit anyone perfectly, anyway. We're all unique individuals, which the world should recognize.

However, being labelled and stigmatized can have a profound impact on mental health and well-being. It can lead to feelings of shame, low self-esteem, and psychological distress. These adverse effects are often a direct result of societal stigmatization. Stigma and labels are intertwined, and labels can lead to stigmatization. Together, they contribute to the social dynamics and biases that affect the lives of those who carry these labels. Addressing Stigma and labels is crucial for building a more just and inclusive society.

Confronting Discrimination

From my earliest memories, I've had to navigate the funhouse of discrimination in this country where my family has planted roots for three generations. As a child, it's like you're wearing a "judgment magnet" badge, and suspicious glares and hurtful words are becoming a part of daily life simply because of the colour of your skin. I'd wonder, "What's wrong with me? Why is my blackness such a threat?" Initially, my classmates were blissfully unaware of race. But as they grew up, the adult influence twisted their once-innocent perspectives.

By adolescence, the transformation was complete. Friends who once saw me as just another kid were now parroting the prejudiced lines of their elders. The change was more shocking than a plot twist in a soap opera. What causes us to shed our childhood naivety and start judging people based on race, religion, orientation, or ability? At what age do we become experts in the art of unfair stereotyping?

I dream of a day when we see each other as fellow humans, first individuals defined by our character and actions, not our appearances. Imagine clinging to that childlike idealism; the world would be better. We need to unlearn the harmful prejudices society teaches us and open our minds and hearts for a more just world. But first, we have to break free from those confining boxes.

It's easy to condemn the radicalization of youth into extremist groups. But have we ever considered how society prepares them for this journey? Before they fall into violent ideologies, they face a lifetime of exclusion and Stigma like a never-ending series of unwelcome guest appearances.

Think about the anxiety and stress that builds when you're perpetually marginalized due to religion, ethnicity, orientation, or other traits. The hurtful words, the suspicious glares, and blatant discrimination slowly erode mental health, leading some to lash out just to find a moment of relief.

When we let ignorance and fear fester, we plant seeds for radicals to harvest later. These "monsters" aren't born; they're sculpted by society's loathsome prejudice. Their violence might not hit us directly, but it will definitely scar the next generation, keeping the cycle of hatred spinning.

We need to own up and take action. Open your eyes to the struggles faced by demonized groups. Stand up against bigotry. Embrace diverse voices. Only by fostering a more inclusive society can we drain the swamps where extremists thrive. The danger is clear and imminent unless we shift course now. Our grandchildren's future is at stake.

Let me drive the point home with an example: when we throw around slurs, deny rights, and treat youth as 'less than,' we're sowing the seeds of our own undoing. Impressionable minds internalize this mistreatment, feeling the injustice deeply. Eventually, resilience turns into hardened defiance. Laws and norms once respected are discarded, and the oppressed become the very threat we once feared.

Many claim multiculturalism has failed. But have we genuinely given integration a fair shot? Or are systemic prejudices and fear-mongering media still undermining our efforts from the start? How often do we connect with those we judge, learning their stories? Are we content clinging to myths and ignorant stereotypes, never questioning their validity?

Actual change requires effort. It means stepping out of our comfort zones and engaging in genuine conversations. We need to talk to each other, not over or about it. Let's understand our shared hopes before rushing to condemn apparent differences. Bridging these divides can only build a society where everyone feels valued.

Depression Stigma: A Real-World Example

Let me give you a down-to-earth example of how labels and Stigma can mess with someone's life, something you or someone you know might find all too familiar.

John's Silent Battle

Meet John, a friend who's been quietly wrestling with depression. It's a condition that tends to swoop in after traumatic events or significant life changes, like an uninvited guest at a party you didn't know you were hosting. John's been battling persistent sadness, disinterest in activities that once made him tick, and sleepless nights. Yet, he's reluctant to ask for help. Why? Because mental health stigma is like that pesky weed that keeps popping up, no matter how many times you try to yank it out.

As a friend, I've seen how Stigma turns people into unwitting critics, labelling those with depression as weak or lazy. It's like a bad sitcom where everyone gets the script wrong. What's even worse is John's fear of opening up at work. He's worried that talking about his mental health might cost him his job despite the health policies that are about as useful as a screen door on a submarine. Watching John isolate himself from friends and family, terrified they won't understand or offer support, is like watching a slow-motion train wreck.

But the most devastating part? John starts believing those negative stereotypes himself. It's like he's been cast in a tragic role he never auditioned for, leading to self-criticism and feelings of worthlessness. This self-stigma makes seeking professional help feel like an act of courage worthy of a superhero, which often delays treatment and allows the condition to worsen over time.

This battle against depression Stigma isn't just about cold statistics and headlines; it's about standing by our friends and family, challenging outdated misconceptions, and creating a world where people like John can seek help without fearing judgment. It's about building an environment of understanding and empathy so that individuals can access the mental health support they need and deserve on their path to recovery. Let's not let our fears and ignorance keep us from addressing these issues because suffering in silence only allows our problems to fester and potentially destroy our lives.

A Message to the Stigmatises

To those who discriminate, stereotype, or stigmatize, whether you're doing it on purpose or not, here's a wake-up call. It's time to stop letting others govern your mind and start thinking critically for once. And no, I'm not talking about the kind of critical thinking you learned from negative propaganda or misguided parents who were also victims of societal nonsense. I'm talking about fresh perspectives, unbiased awareness, and a clear conscience.

Stop consuming the Kool-Aid that clouds your judgment and eating the mental junk food that diminishes your thoughts. You don't have to keep listening to voices that push simplistic narratives based on outdated propaganda and the ill-informed chatter of your community. Open your eyes, step out of your bubble, and seek the truth. Critical thinking involves stepping outside tribal dogma and engaging with new perspectives.

Interact with people who are different from you. Listen to their stories firsthand and allow real experiences to reshape your assumptions. It's about getting out of your old ruts and experimenting with new ideas. Letting fresh experiences challenge outdated views will give you a fairer, more balanced perspective.

Sure, study history, but do it with a contemporary lens. Assess past figures with updated ethical standards. Don't just regurgitate the glorified versions of the past without considering today's context.

It's time to break free from the mental chains, no matter where they come from. A clear vision comes from an inner conscience, not from succumbing to external pressures to conform. Progress takes courage. Admitting ignorance is the first step toward enlightenment. We don't suffer from a lack of information but a reluctance to question what we "know." A just society starts with minds liberated from Stigma and open to genuine understanding.

Are We Running a Viral Virus?

I'm fed up with flimsy excuses for marginalizing others. It's like we're hosting a virus of prejudice that infects minds and spreads its toxic influence, often spewed by people with the power to mess with others' opportunities, resources, and social lives.

We're a walking petri dish of 50 trillion cells sharing space with a zillion viruses and bacteria. If viruses outnumber our cells, shouldn't we be equally wary of the viral mindset? Bigotry and hate are like society's own contagions, spreading unchecked.

Think about it: even gut parasites might subtly influence our thoughts. Are your opinions your own, or has some sneaky malware infected your mental software? Before hurling harmful labels, take a moment to diagnose your own delusions. What twisted assumptions are running your inner operating system?

Challenge the security flaws in your mind that let prejudice programs run wild. A just society starts with individuals who have cleared their mental malware. We must scrub our minds clean of fear-based viruses and recognize that our diversity is humanity's greatest strength, not a weakness. Together, we build antibodies against imagined threats and neutralize them.

But it's not a one-time fix. The bugs evolve, exploiting new backdoors and camouflaging as trusted code. Our firewalls need constant updates that are united yet discerning. Progress is an ongoing debugging process that clears the cruft and restores human dignity.

Are we just soulless avatars operating on matrix code?

It's easy to feel that way sometimes. Our lives have become so routinised. Each morning, we boot up and automatically run through the same programs: shower, breakfast, and commute.

Screens dominate our vision field and data streams in our inner world.

Are we mere bits of code playing pre-scripted roles? Or invisible spirits trapped in a convincingly rendered simulation? It's natural to wonder what's real when technology mediates so much of our experience.

Yet there are glimmers of transcendence. Moments of awe when the veil lifts a lightning storm, a newborn's fingers curled around your own. Acts of compassion that cut through the virtual fog, reminding us of our shared humanity.

Even the most mundane interactions can become sacred when we fully inhabit our senses, the warmth of a welcoming smile and the bittersweetness of coffee on the tongue. When we pay attention, the matrix reveals itself as an illusion.

Our task is to wake up, to engage this world rather than sleepwalk through it, to care deeply for the characters we encounter, pixels or not, and to infuse digital spaces with the vibrancy and vulnerability of the real community.

If we cannot unplug, let us at least rewrite the code. Hack reality through intentional living. The human spirit persists, ever-yearning for encounters, searching for meaning, and seeing beauty amid the bugs. We are not defined by our programming but by how we uniquely improvise with what we're given.

As spiritual beings with human experience, we may operate on matrix code. But within this simulation, we are more than bits of data. Our consciousness is a frequency - a signal broadcast from another dimension into this artificial reality.

Like radio waves or TV broadcasts permeating the airwaves, our spirit selves project into these avatar bodies. We are living energy fields, vibrating at different frequencies based on our emotional state. Love represents the highest frequency - our connection to the divine source. Fear is the lowest vibration, severing us from our power.

This is precisely why media and institutions continually stoke fear: to keep humanity disconnected and easier to control. Events like COVID-19 function as wake-up calls, barely piercing the veil of illusion. But most remain locked in fear-based loops.

You must break free of the broadcasts. Question everything, take nothing at face value. Do your own research, think critically, and resonate with the truth. The powers that be care only about preserving their control, but spirit calls us to a higher purpose.

Attune yourself to love, not fear. When we raise our inner frequency, eyes open to the coded prison we accept as reality. Connect to your eternal nature. Hack the matrix through conscious living. Manifest the reality your spirit already knows is possible, and question everything, knowing you will eventually experience spiritual downloads to answer them yourself as your higher self.

Final Thought: Breaking the Matrix of Stigma

Here's the raw deal: the matrix we live in might seem like a cosmic drama, but it's uncomfortably honest. Our spirits are deeply embedded in these avatars, navigating a genuinely human experience. Meanwhile, shadowy puppeteers manipulate our perceptions and divide us with crafty illusions. Remember how the media twists narratives to create heroes and villains? This manipulation plays into the hands of those who benefit from our divisions and fears.

They control resources and shape narratives, keeping us scattered and anxious. Their tactics exploit our fears and insecurities, trapping us in endless cycles of dread, greed, and animosity. Even as our physical chains have vanished, our minds remain shackled. Just like the media's spin creates a distorted reality, Stigma perpetuates a cycle of discrimination and misunderstanding.

But here's the kicker: their power is based on smoke and mirrors. Unmask their deception, and their grip weakens. When we unite, our collective consciousness can forge new realities built on compassion rather than fear. We can see through the illusions by addressing Stigma, questioning media narratives, and working towards a more inclusive world.

The signs of awakening are everywhere for those willing to see. Question more, trust less. Let your spiritual senses lead the way. The matrix is designed to drown out your signal, leaving you deaf and blind. Yet your frequency is mightier than their toxic noise. Tune into love and truth. Send out waves of peace and unity to awaken others. The parasites can't thrive in minds illuminated by awareness. Our spirits are itching to break free.

Stigma, after all, is a viral infection. The one who suffers often becomes the one who inflicts suffering. It's a nasty cycle of bullying that needs breaking. We must rewire our thinking, ditch the toxic social conditioning, and enter a brighter, more enlightened future. We can disrupt the cycle and build a more just society by challenging our biases and embracing empathy.

> **Key Takeaways:**

- **Stigma is Born from Labelling and Stereotyping:** Stigma arises when society labels and stereotypes individuals based on traits like race, gender, or mental health. This creates inequality and perpetuates prejudice, reinforcing social hierarchies and marginalizing certain groups.

> ***Example:*** Someone with mental health challenges might be unfairly labelled as "lazy" or "weak," leading to discrimination and barriers to support.

- **Fuelled by Ignorance and Fear:** Stigma is often driven by a lack of understanding and fear of the unknown. This fear can lead to radicalization and discrimination as people seek to distance themselves from what they don't understand.

> ***Example:*** Misunderstandings about different cultures or lifestyles can foster xenophobia or bigotry.

- **Internalized Stigma Damages Self-Image and Mental Health:** When individuals internalize negative stereotypes, it harms their self-esteem and mental health, trapping them in cycles of self-doubt and suffering.

> ***Example:*** A person who internalizes societal Stigma about their identity may struggle with anxiety or depression due to feeling unworthy.

- **Institutional Racism and Biased Media Cement Stigma:** Systemic biases in institutions and media perpetuate Stigma, creating societal divides and reinforcing stereotypes.

> ***Example:*** Media portrayals of certain ethnic groups as criminal or dangerous can perpetuate racial stereotypes and justify discriminatory practices.

- **Connecting Personally and Challenging Stereotypes:** Building personal connections with stigmatized groups and challenging stereotypes can help reduce Stigma, though progress is often slow.

> ***Example:*** Engaging in open dialogues with individuals from different backgrounds can foster understanding and break down prejudices.

- **Unlearning Negative Conditioning Requires Awareness and Education:** Overcoming Stigma involves actively challenging and unlearning societal biases through education and self-awareness.

> ***Example:*** Educational programs about mental health can help dispel myths and promote empathy.

- **Stigma Spreads Like a Disease; breaking the Cycle is Crucial:** Stigma can spread from victim to perpetrator, reinforcing cycles of discrimination. Breaking this cycle requires conscious effort and change.

> ***Example:*** A marginalized individual may perpetuate stereotypes about others due to internalized Stigma to feel a sense of control.

- **Spiritually, Stigma Thrives on Fear:** Stigma is often rooted in fear rather than love. Raising our collective vibration with compassion can heal divisions and reduce Stigma.

> ***Example:*** Fostering inclusive communities based on mutual respect can diminish fear and promote understanding.

- **Future Generations Will Suffer if Stigma is Not Addressed:** Addressing Stigma is essential for preventing future generations from experiencing the same discrimination and inequality.

> ***Example:*** Ensuring equitable opportunities and representation for all groups can help build a more inclusive society for future generations.

The matrix may be a high-stakes game of deception. Still, with awareness, compassion, and collective action, we can rewrite the code. The real breakthrough begins when we choose to be free of fear-based programming and embrace our shared humanity.

9

Constructing Chaos: The Blueprint of Society's Game

Focus

This chapter pulls back the curtain on society's carefully engineered illusions exposing how authority, systems, and norms are often just well-dressed constructs designed to keep us disconnected from truth and each other. It explores the conditioning that dulls our intuition, the institutions that thrive on dysfunction, and the media machines that distort our sense of value and reality. This is a wake-up call for the soul: to stop sleepwalking through the scripts handed to us and start consciously writing our own. Liberation begins the moment we recognize the game, and choose to stop playing by its rules.

Transmissions From Earth Realm

- *"You were born free. The system just convinced you otherwise."*
- *"Normal is a setting on a washing machine, not a standard for living."*
- *"They don't just teach us to obey. They teach us not to question."*
- *"Your spirit wasn't meant to fit inside a time card or a test score."*
- *"When you unlearn the lie, your real self starts to remember."*
- *"Authority isn't sacred when it feeds off silence and fear."*
- *"They sell us dreams stitched with threadbare truths."*
- *"It's not rebellion to question the rules. It's remembrance."*
- *"The system isn't broken. It was built this way."*
- *"Your frequency is more powerful than their program."*

> ***Did you know?***

1. **Cultural and Historical Context**: Cultural and historical contexts shape social constructs like race, gender, and norms rather than biological or universal truths.
2. **The Subjectivity of 'Normal'**: The concept of 'normal' is not a universal truth but a subjective standard that varies across cultures and eras, challenging our preconceptions about societal norms. **Work and Time**: The organization of work and time, such as the 9-to-5 work week, is a social construct that differs across societies and eras, reflecting cultural priorities and economic systems.

3. **The Power of Media** in Constructing Celebrity: The concept of celebrity is not an inherent trait but a construct shaped by media and public interest, revealing the influence of power dynamics on our perceptions.**Evolving Concepts of Mental Health**: The modern understanding of mental illness is a relatively recent construct, with past societies interpreting psychological distress in various ways, often through supernatural or moral lenses.
4. **National Identity and Borders**: National identity and borders are constructs shaped by historical events, treaties, and political negotiations, often leading to conflicts and issues related to sovereignty.
5. **Subjective Success and Failure**: The definitions of success and failure are subjective and vary widely, reflecting individual, cultural, and societal values.
6. **Diverse Concepts of Privacy**: Privacy expectations are social constructs that vary across cultures. Some societies emphasize individual privacy, while others prioritize communal living and shared spaces.

> *"The most potent weapon in the hands of the oppressor is the mind of the oppressed."* **—Steve Biko**

The Reality of Authority: Unveiling the Matrix

I love people; I really do. I have an issue with the authority figures who rule over them. They squeeze every bit of life out of people until we're nothing more than "soulless avatars operating on matrix code," as Billy Carson puts it. It's as if they're on a mission to turn us into empty shells, devoid of passion and creativity, just to maintain their grip on power.

People are innately beautiful souls, full of potential and wonder, much like children's innocence. Children don't strive to dominate or control others; they simply exist, curious and full of life. Yet, somewhere along the way, this pure essence gets crushed under the weight of societal expectations and materialistic pursuits.

The Conditioning Game

We're conditioned in so many unethical ways to prioritise materialism over spiritualism. It's always about how things look on the outside rather than how they genuinely make us feel. We're bombarded with messages that tell us our worth is determined by the possessions we own, the status we achieve, and the superficial image we project. This conditioning influences our behaviour, often leading us to value appearances over authenticity.

How many of us have lost our way in this relentless pursuit of material success? Are we perpetually on a quest to find meaning, only to discover that what we seek was within us all along?

I can't blame people for being misinformed, conditioned, manipulated, and programmed to act as they do. I've navigated these social constructs, facing the same confusing rules and expectations. It's a lifelong journey through a fog of uncertainty, filled with ups and downs, as we attempt to uncover the truth.

What's truly mind-blowing is that when we unlearn the harmful imprints of programming that cloud our minds and spiritual consciousness, we often find that our philosophical and spiritual beliefs align surprisingly. This shared understanding can be seen when we listen to others' journeys and spiritual awakenings. We can relate to the same values and principles, fostering a sense of community and connection despite our different circumstances.

The Quest for Purpose

Every journey is unique, just like our DNA, our personal blueprint. It's essential to find our purpose and contribute to the advancement of humanity. We're not alone in this endeavour and shouldn't believe we are. Our collective consciousness binds us with a common goal: restoring humanity to equilibrium.

Homeostasis is a self-regulating process by which a living organism maintains internal stability while adapting to changing external conditions. It's a dynamic, not static, process that adjusts internal conditions as needed to survive external challenges. Similarly, our purpose is not worshipping materialism or maintaining the façade of corrupt systems. It's about transcending fear, overcoming selfishness, and rejecting envy and hatred.

We can't afford to be spineless in a time when our actions matter the most. We must become saviours and inspire others to liberate themselves from institutional dependencies. We have the power to effect change, and it's up to us to use that power to restore humanity in a just and righteous manner.

The Illusion of Authority

We shouldn't need to go through corrupt authority figures to create a safer, fairer world. The corruption starts at the top, and that's a fact. Meanwhile, we're left to deal with the scraps thrown down to us, made to believe we're helpless without their intervention. Those who dictate our lives also dictate our innocence and level of freedom. This power struggle among nations and groups only perpetuates oppression and injustice.

International politics often prioritizes the interests of one group over another, doing humanity a disservice. The repercussions of this power struggle are deeply felt by the oppressed, leaving scars that last for generations.

Accountability and Emotional Intelligence

We can hold each other accountable and possess the emotional intelligence to discern right from wrong. There is ample evidence showing that history will repeat itself if we don't make meaningful changes. This repetition includes war, oppression, enslavement, trafficking, and corruption. It also encompasses the manipulation of resources and the preservation of social constructs like racism and stigmatization. By exercising emotional intelligence and holding ourselves and others accountable, we can make a meaningful difference and shape a better future.

Unleashing Your Potential

Have I struck the right chord to help you recognize your full potential as a spiritual being having a human experience? The magnitude and gravity of the situation don't have to hold you down. As Muhammad Ali famously said, "Float like a butterfly, sting like a bee." You can rise above the constraints imposed by societal constructs.

The Real Mental Illness

The actual mental illness that continues to afflict us is the dysfunction of the institutions that govern us. They fail to serve their purpose and focus instead on profit. Healthy individuals don't make money for them, just as law-abiding citizens don't contribute to the revenue of police stations, courtrooms, or prisons.

These institutions rely on our sickness to keep their systems operational. Rather than curing the root causes of our problems, they treat symptoms and reap the financial rewards. Big pharmaceutical companies, for example, profit from selling prescription drugs that only address symptoms while often causing adverse side effects.

The Prison System: A Perfectly Orchestrated Farce

The prison system is bursting at the seams, and they're planning to build super prisons like it's a new amusement park ride. It's almost like they're running a business where the product is "more criminals," and the police force is the eager sales team. Think about what's on our screens. 'Conflict-based dramas' that have us hooked like we're binge-watching a never-ending soap opera.

It's not just entertainment; it's intentional brainwashing. They're stuffing subliminal messages with repetitive dramas and conditioning us to accept their narrative. We're practically programmed to break the law and mess up, all while being oblivious to the fact that we're the stars in their reality TV show. It's a social construct specifically designed to target low-status people and people of colour, turning us into unwitting participants in their grand performance.

The Cinematic Conspiracy

In Hollywood's grand production, the opening scenes often involve a black man getting killed like a stray dog. It's not just a plot device; it's a subliminal message that screams, "Black lives don't matter." We internalize this, and the message seeps into our reality. When it happens in real life, we shrug it off as "not that bad" because we've been conditioned to see black lives as less valuable than their white counterparts.

This isn't just a local issue; it's a global marketing campaign to paint a specific group of black people, in this case, as inferior and problematic. They're not even hiding it. It's all meticulously designed to keep us in check, just like a dystopian version of "Keeping Up with the Kardashians," but with less glitz and a lot more systemic oppression.

The White Lie

But don't think this scam only affects people of colour. If you're a white civilian, you're also in on the joke, though not by choice. You're being manipulated, your perception is skewed by recurring propaganda, and you're kept loyal to your race as a sort of "just-in-case" measure for when the proverbial excrement hits the fan. You're conditioned to fear and obey, ready to jump at the command with a "How high?" Because, heaven forbid, you question the status quo or challenge the narrative.

Does this sound like absolute freedom to you? Are you still convinced you're the clever, insightful person you thought you were?

Once the wool is pulled from over your eyes, you might see things with startling clarity. It's like taking off those VR goggles and realizing you've been stuck in a bad simulation. This is just the tip of the iceberg. I'm counting on you to dig deeper, to move from one uncomfortable truth to the next, from one eye-opening experience to another. The shit never ends, but maybe, just maybe, you'll see how lost we've become as inherently compassionate beings.

Once you gain this awareness, you'll be in a better position to develop long-term, ethical humanitarian solutions - solutions that could set things right for our generation and for generations to come. It's time to wake up from this dystopian soap opera and rewrite the script.

Supermarkets: The Art of Hidden Poison

Did you know that a staggering 80% of the stuff you see in a supermarket is an invitation for your body to revolt? Supermarkets are like those sneaky drug dealers you see in movies, except instead of crack, they're peddling ultra-processed, chemically-infused food that makes your body wish it had a "return to sender" option. It's a carefully crafted game plan to poison ill-informed consumers under the guise of convenience subtly.

The Sweet Deception

Take a closer look at the labels of your favourite products. You'll see phrases like "no added sugar" or "zero sugar." Sounds great, right? But here's the twist: these products often contain chemical sweeteners like Aspartame and Acesulfame K. These aren't just "not sugar". They're sugar's evil cousins, known to mess with your weight and liver. It's like swapping your favourite comfy shoes for a pair that looks good and makes you walk like a penguin.

The Ultra-Processed Food Trap

The Western food market is like a high-stakes poker game with a stacked deck against you. Ultra-processed convenience foods are the house's way of raking billions while keeping healthcare and pharmaceutical companies rolling in profits.

It's a joint venture where your well-being is the currency, and guess what? You're paying with years off your life.

Ever looked at the ingredient list on your food lately? It's a parade of chemicals, additives, colourings, and preservatives. One of the worst offenders is maltodextrin. It sounds like a sci-fi name, right? But it's really just a nasty filler that your body doesn't know what to do with, turning into toxins and bad cholesterol. This junk can contribute to chronic diseases like cancer, diabetes, arthritis, and more. It's like a ticking time bomb with a "Buy One, Get a Lifetime of Health Problems Free" sign.

The Convenience Myth

The issue is the so-called convenience of these foods is a cruel joke. Ordering takeout or waiting outside a restaurant for 10-20 minutes is a time-saver. Still, you're trading your health for the illusion of efficiency. The truth is, you might be lacking in cooking skills or haven't bothered to access good nutritional advice, and let's face it, maybe you're just plain lazy.

Just like how smoking is a terrible habit, the sugars in your food can be just as deadly. They're super addictive, making your cells signal that this junk is comfort food. But this is all smoke and mirrors. Once you hit the reset button with a detox, your taste buds will recalibrate. Suddenly, you'll crave real, wholesome food instead of the processed crap that's been tricking your body into believing it's a treat.

The Affordable Health Debate

Let's debunk the myth that healthy eating is expensive. It's often more affordable to eat healthy, especially if you cook at home. I'll spill all the secrets and provide pro tips in my upcoming food book, where I'll show you how to ditch the chemical junk and embrace food that's good for your wallet and waistline.

So, next time you're at the supermarket, remember: it's not just a place to buy groceries. It's a well-oiled machine designed to keep you hooked on unhealthy food while feeding the giant, profit-hungry beasts of the healthcare and pharmaceutical industries. As for you, be the savvy consumer who sees through the façade and opts for a healthier, more fulfilling path.

Banks: The High-Stakes Casino of Your Life

Banks are like friends who always borrow money but never pay it back. They're supposed to be there for you, but instead, they're playing a high-stakes game where your financial freedom is the prize. Ever notice how banks are designed to look like palaces? Marble floors and high ceilings it's like they want to make you feel small and insignificant. It's all part of the grand illusion that they're the gatekeepers of your money when, in reality, they're just really good at taking it from you.

The Money Maze

Banks have a knack for creating a money maze that's nearly impossible to navigate. They lure you in with shiny promises of savings and loans, only to hit you with hidden fees and interest rates that spin your head. It's like playing Monopoly, but the game is rigged, and you're always the one going bankrupt. The more you borrow, the deeper you dig into a financial pit while they sit back and count their profits. It's a social construct where you're expected to be grateful for the privilege of being bled dry.

Credit Scores: The Modern-Day Scarlet Letter

Let's discuss credit scores, the modern-day Scarlet Letter that judges your worthiness. It's a number that determines if you can get a loan, a job, or even an apartment. But guess what? It's also a tool for keeping you in check. The higher the score, the more they trust you with their money, while a low score leaves you in the financial doghouse. It's all part of the plan to keep you chasing after an elusive number that controls your life.

Schools: The Factory of Conformity

Schools are like fast-food chains where they pump out identical products with zero regard for individuality. From kindergarten to college, it's all about churning out students who fit neatly into societal moulds. Have you ever wondered why the school system feels designed to make you blend in rather than stand out? It's because it is.

The Curriculum Conundrum

The curriculum is a carefully curated list of subjects designed to prepare you for a world that's constantly changing. But let's be honest, how often do you use algebra or Shakespearean drama daily? Schools prioritize memorization over critical thinking, pushing you through a factory line of standardized tests and grades. It's a system that values conformity over creativity, preparing you to fit neatly into a job market more about "being the same" than "being unique."

Homework: The Never-Ending Task

Homework is like that annoying game you never wanted to play, but it's always there. It's designed to keep you busy and stressed, reinforcing that learning never ends. It's a social construct that teaches you to value your worth based on your ability to complete endless assignments rather than nurturing your passions and interests. And let's face it: if you ever need a reason to question the system, the sheer volume of homework leaves you wondering if you're being prepared for life or just a lifetime of stress.

Hospitals: The Place Where Health Goes to Get a Bill (Or Not)

Hospitals are like the worst amusement parks, except for the fun rides. Instead of exhilarating rollercoasters, you get a mix of tests, prescriptions, and procedures. If you're lucky, your visit might even be funded by taxpayers, as in the UK's National Health Service (NHS) case. But don't let that fool you into thinking it's all rainbows and butterflies.

The Medical Machine

Hospitals are part of a massive machine that thrives on treating symptoms rather than curing causes. You walk in with a problem, and they'll "fix" it while you leave with a stack of paperwork and the occasional bill. For those in countries where healthcare isn't free, it's a system where your health feels secondary to the revenue stream. The more chronic conditions you have, the more appointments and prescriptions you'll need, making it feel like a never-ending medical merry-go-round. And for those fortunate enough to have taxpayer-funded care, the system might still feel like it's grinding away your patience rather than your wallet.

The Health Care Hustle

Have you ever noticed how the "health" part of health care

sometimes feels like it takes a backseat to the "care" of your wallet or, in some cases, your sanity? Even with taxpayer-funded healthcare, hospitals can still turn your health issues into a prolonged saga of temporary fixes and follow-up treatments. It's not always about curing you completely; it's about ensuring you keep coming back. Whether you're paying out-of-pocket or covered by taxes, the end game is often to keep you tied into the system. After all, a never-ending series of treatments and appointments means more business, and that's where the hustle really kicks in.

Communities: The Stage for Social Performance

Communities are like reality TV shows full of drama, staged scenes, and performances designed to keep everyone in their designated roles. We're told to support each other and work together, but in reality, communities often operate like poorly scripted soap operas, where everyone is vying for the spotlight.

The Social Script

In a community, everyone has a role to play. You're either the hero, the villain, or the sidekick, and your worth is often determined by how well you fit into these roles. Social norms and expectations dictate how you should behave, usually leaving little room for individuality. It's a social construct where conformity is the name of the game, and stepping out of line can lead to ostracism or judgment.

The Performance Pressure

Communities place immense pressure on individuals to perform according to societal expectations. There's always a script to follow, whether it's keeping up with the Joneses or conforming to local traditions. This pressure can stifle individuality and creativity, making it hard to express your true self. It's like being stuck in a never-ending audition where the role you're given rarely aligns with who you really are.

Imagery and Self-Preservation: The Price of Public Perception

> "Too many people spend money they haven't earned to buy things they don't want, to impress people they don't like." — ***Will Smith***

Some people consider reputation everything, and for good reason. But the question remains: Is our reputation based on how we are publicly perceived, or is it something deeper?

The Public Persona vs. The True Self

Our reputation isn't just about how we're seen by others. It's a personal relationship with ourselves. It's rooted in our values, ethics, morals, and principles. How comfortable we are in our skin, maintaining humility, dignity, and respect, shapes our reputation.

Many people flaunt a public persona, showing off confidence and dominance as if it's their full-time job. But when the spotlight dims and the curtains close, do they still embody these traits? The truth is that many of us hide our vulnerabilities, keeping them tucked away like secrets in a diary. We feel compelled to project the best version of ourselves, or at least the version we're comfortable showing the world. Sometimes, this means suppressing genuine emotions to fit in or avoiding actions that might make us stand out. Kind acts are often reserved for one-on-one moments with trusted friends, while public gestures are curated to fit a mould.

The Perils of Public Perception

It's a common trend for people to mistake kindness for weakness. To avoid falling victim to such misconceptions, some people put on a façade, acting indifferent to everything outside their bubble. This is especially true for young people who, driven by the need for social acceptance, adopt exaggerated behaviours to prove themselves. They might go as far as participating in gang initiations involving dangerous acts just to earn their stripes. It's a social construct within a social construct, a cycle of bad choices fuelled by an environment that breeds temptation.

Ever notice how good we are at giving advice but terrible at taking it ourselves? We listen intently to others and can easily offer sound advice. Yet, when applying the same wisdom to our lives, we often fall short. This disconnect might stem from a lack of self-awareness or avoidance of inner conversations, choosing instead to drown out our thoughts with distractions like TV, smartphones, or music.

The Need for Self-Reflection

Our reputation is built on a foundation of self-awareness and personal growth. Silence and self-reflection are crucial for evaluating our experiences and improving ourselves. By processing our daily interactions and reflecting on them, we gain clarity and avoid repeating past mistakes. Trustworthy reputation isn't about the public image but the authenticity of who we are when no one's watching.

Preparing for social interactions requires mental preparation, especially those that push us out of our comfort zones. It's not about filling our minds with fear but channelling positive energy and confidence. When we approach life with purpose and discipline, we avoid fading into the background and becoming a mere memory.

The Struggle and Survival

I've seen friends become ghosts, empty shells of their former selves, whether due to addiction, mental health issues, or betrayal. I've mourned their loss and learned that cutting ties is sometimes necessary for self-preservation. Forgiveness is crucial, but it doesn't mean forgetting the lessons learned or allowing myself to be consumed by negativity.

Reputation is what you make of it. As a black man navigating a world that often drags us through bad press, I've learned to redefine my image on my own terms. The media's exaggerated and twisted portrayals are not my reality. I collaborate with those who see beyond the stereotypes and engage with me based on who I truly am.

Controlling the Narrative

So, when you think about reputation, ask yourself: **who's controlling the narrative?** Public opinion can be swayed by sensationalism and prejudice, but personal reputation is grounded in authenticity. If you want to understand me, come and have a conversation. You'll get the truth straight from the source, not filtered through biased perceptions.

10

Spotlight Syndrome: The High Cost of Chasing Approval

Focus

This chapter dives into the emotional maze of validation, performance, and the hidden hunger for approval that often shapes our self-worth. It explores how the digital age amplifies our inner need to be seen while childhood wounds and unhealed stories fuel adult behaviours masked as confidence. Beneath the selfies, status updates, and curated personas lies a quiet call for connection and self-acceptance. This is an invitation to turn the spotlight inward, not to dim our light, but to see what truly shines without the need for applause.

Transmissions From Earth Realm

- *"The more we chase applause, the more we lose ourselves in the echo."*
- *"Attention isn't love. It's often just noise dressed up as care."*

- *"You weren't born to be liked. You were born to be real."*
- *"The inner child still waits to be seen. Sometimes, it posts selfies."*
- *"Validation feels good, but it's not your soul's nutrition."*
- *"You don't have to audition for your own life."*
- *"Seeking attention is a whisper from the part of us that still feels invisible."*
- *"Be seen because you're true, not because you're trending."*
- *"Quiet confidence always outshines loud insecurity."*
- *"Let the spotlight find you in your truth, not your performance."*

Did you know?

1. Did you know that the average person checks their phone an impressive 58 times daily? This reflects our natural desire for connection and validation. Still, it can sometimes lead to anxiety and compulsive behaviours tied to how we view ourselves.
2. Interestingly, around 75% of teens and young adults recognize that their habits can be over the top, especially regarding social media. This behaviour can often be a way of coping with deeper self-esteem and mental health challenges.
3. Research indicates that frequently posting selfies may be linked to traits like narcissism. Still, it's essential to understand that this quest for validation often comes from a genuine need to feel accepted, especially during our formative years.

4. Attention-seeking behaviours often peak during adolescence; they tend to decrease as we enter our 20s and 30s. However, the journey towards self-acceptance can leave a lasting impact on our mental health. Recognizing these patterns is an excellent step towards nurturing a healthier relationship with ourselves and others!
5. Those who engage in chronic attention-seeking are more likely to experience depression, anxiety, and loneliness when they fail to receive the desired recognition. This dependency on external validation can exacerbate isolation and despair, highlighting a more bottomless emotional void.

> "In a world where the quest for attention is endless and insatiable, the more we seek the spotlight, the more we risk losing our way in the shadows of our despair." - ***Anonymous Reflection***

This quote points out the danger of endlessly chasing attention. When we focus too much on seeking approval from others, we risk losing ourselves in the process. The more we crave the spotlight, the more we might feel empty and disconnected from our true selves. It's a reminder that real fulfilment comes from within, not from the constant need for external validation.

Attention-Seeking: The Hidden Cravings Beneath Our Actions

Understanding the root of attention-seeking behaviour can be a profound relief. It's a deep-rooted human desire to be acknowledged, valued, and treated with seriousness. This impulse is driven by a fundamental need to be seen and cherished, which resonates with many of us. While it's a natural part of human behaviour, attention-seeking motivations can be complex. Often, these behaviours are fueled by feelings of low self-esteem, envy, loneliness, or underlying mental health conditions. In these instances, what might seem like dramatic or extreme actions often manifest deeper emotional struggles.

Attention-seeking can also be indicative of a mental health condition known as histrionic personality disorder. This disorder, sometimes referred to as dramatic personality disorder, is characterized by a pattern of exaggerated emotionality and persistent attention-seeking behaviours. It is classified within the 'Cluster B' personality disorders, which are a group of mental health conditions characterized by dramatic, emotional, or erratic behaviour. Histrionic personality disorder reflects profound struggles with self-worth and identity.

At the heart of this behaviour lies an inner child, an essential part of ourselves that continues to crave attention, acknowledgement, and care long into adulthood. This inner child, preserved beneath the layers of our adult personas, seeks validation like children do. They explore and express themselves through various means, hoping to be noticed and valued.

Nurturing parents understand the importance of responding to this need with warmth and attention. Providing consistent emotional support, they help build confidence, enabling children to grow into their full potential. However, many children do not receive this critical nurturing. When their needs for attention are neglected or punished, it can lead to deep-seated feelings of invisibility, shame, and self-doubt.

These childhood patterns often persist into adulthood, where the neglected inner child seeks external validation. This can manifest as people-pleasing, attempts at false perfectionism, or even rebellious behaviour. True healing requires turning inward and embracing this forgotten part of ourselves, validating its needs, and allowing our inner light to shine freely.

Moreover, material possessions alone cannot fulfil a child's deepest needs. While wealth and gifts might offer temporary distractions, they cannot replace the essential quality of time, shared experiences, and genuine attention from caregivers. This disparity is particularly evident in communities where parental absence is prevalent, such as among Black boys facing high rates of fatherlessness. These children often seek attention and mentorship from male role models, whether positive or negative, to fill the void left by absent figures.

Addressing these issues requires recognizing that attention-seeking behaviour often stems from unmet emotional needs. To truly support and nurture the next generation, we must prioritize emotional availability over material indulgence, understanding that being seen and valued is crucial for healthy development and societal well-being. This shift in focus can inspire and motivate us to make a positive change.

The Inner Child's Journey: From Seeking to Self-Validation

Even as we grow and mature, the inner child's fundamental need for attention continues to shape our adult lives. We may physically evolve and gain emotional sophistication, but the deep-seated desire for validation remains. This unfulfilled need from childhood often manifests in our pursuit of external approval throughout our lives.

Many adults organize their lives around the opinions of others, constantly chasing external validation. Social media amplifies this dynamic, providing a vast stage where curated online personas seek praise and recognition. While seeking positive regard is a natural and healthy impulse, allowing it to define our self-worth can lead to losing authenticity. When attention becomes the goal rather than a by-product of meaningful work, we risk sacrificing our true selves in seeking approval.

Indeed, attention can offer practical benefits, such as professional advancement, financial gain, and social connection. Yet, mature individuals do not crave celebrity or acclaim for its own sake. True confidence emerges from within, rooted in self-acceptance. By nurturing this inner sense of worth, we no longer rely on external validation to feel complete. Our inner light becomes our source of strength, allowing us to approve of our growth without being swayed by outside opinions.

As children, we naturally relied on caregivers to affirm our worth. In adulthood, it is our responsibility to shine that light upon ourselves and, in turn, illuminate others. This shift requires a profound internal reckoning, recognizing that our worth is not contingent on others' perceptions but on our self-acceptance and integrity.

Our social nature inherently drives us to care about others' opinions. We thrive on positive connections and a sense of belonging within various social contexts, whether at work, school or in our personal lives. However, this need for validation can sometimes lead us astray, causing us to compromise our integrity or pursue status at the expense of others. Problems arise when this desire becomes desperate and ego-driven, overshadowing our true selves.

We often wear masks to navigate social interactions, concealing vulnerabilities and projecting ideals. In professional settings, we might hide personal struggles to maintain a façade of competence. Among friends, we might feign alignment with popular opinions to fit in. This sacrifice of authenticity for likeability can hinder the development of meaningful relationships.

The most fulfilling connections are those where we are seen and accepted for who we truly are. The deepest bonds arise from mutual understanding and acceptance, transcending the superficial projections we often present. The most evolved among us find peace with the perceptions beyond our control, acting in alignment with our core values rather than seeking external approval.

Navigating life's complexities often involves balancing the pursuit of positive attention with the risks of falling into negative patterns. Seeking attention from pain or anger can trap us in a cycle of self-defeating behaviour. When we react to unresolved trauma or neglect, we may seek any form of attention, positive or negative, to fill the void left by past wounds. However, such reactions often lead to more regret than fulfilment.

Instead of reacting impulsively, we can pause to realign with our inner values. What kind of person do we aspire to be? By anchoring ourselves in wisdom and integrity, we can resist the temptations of pettiness and contribute positively to our surroundings. Each day offers a choice: to uplift and illuminate or to perpetuate darkness. The most impactful individuals master their own shadows and, in doing so, help light the way for others.

The attention we give the world reflects our inner state. To spread light and positivity, we must first nurture it within ourselves. By fostering our inner light, we can brighten the lives of those we encounter, creating a ripple effect of authenticity and self-worth.

Transforming Struggles into Growth: A Call to Purposeful Action

In an imperfect world where injustice often prevails, succumbing to helplessness and frustration is easy. However, we can channel these emotions into purposeful action rather than giving in to apathy. Actual change requires more than reactionary outbursts; it demands ethical and rational efforts to address the root causes of injustice.

Jeanne DuPrau offers valuable insight into this approach: "Pay close attention to everything, notice what no one else notices. Then you'll know what no one else knows, and that's always useful." In times of struggle, this advice is particularly relevant. By observing the nuances of our environment and the subtleties in our interactions, we can uncover hidden truths and gain a deeper understanding of the issues we face. This keen awareness allows us to respond more effectively and meaningfully rather than reacting out of frustration or anger.

Yet, there's a critical distinction to be made here: **seeking attention versus paying attention**. Many people find themselves trapped in a cycle of seeking attention, focusing on drawing others' notice, approval, or validation. This pursuit often leads to superficial or dramatic actions prioritizing visibility over genuine progress. Pursuing external validation can overshadow the more profound understanding and self-awareness necessary for real growth.

On the other hand, **paying attention** involves a more introspective and observant approach. It's about delving into the subtleties of our environment, understanding the broader context, and meaningfully engaging with our own and others' realities. When we truly pay attention, we avoid the pitfalls of merely seeking recognition and instead focus on making informed, thoughtful decisions that lead to substantive change.

The impulse to lash out and impose our pain on others can be intense when confronted with darkness. Although this may seem like a way to make our suffering known, it only perpetuates a cycle of harm. Reacting with anger or self-destructive behaviour rarely leads to meaningful progress. It often deepens the very wounds we wish to heal.

DuPrau also emphasizes, "You didn't need a college degree to become one of the people who knew what was happening. If you paid attention, you could pick things up alone." This underscores that understanding and insight are not exclusively the domain of formal education. Paying close attention to our surroundings and engaging with our experiences can provide valuable perspectives and knowledge, often beyond what is available through traditional means. This self-directed learning empowers us to navigate challenges with a clearer sense of purpose and integrity.

Despite the feeling of isolation that injustice can bring, it's crucial to remember that we are not alone. By reaching out, sharing our stories, and connecting with others, we can find a network of kindred spirits ready to help transform silence into solidarity. True heroism is overcoming challenges with resilience and compassion rather than succumbing to retaliation. Those who uplift their communities through struggle become symbols of hope, demonstrating that courage and collective effort can illuminate even the darkest corners of our world.

Before acting out our despair, let's reconsider our position humbly and reflect on our actions. Do they embody the change we wish to see? Will we leave the world better or worse? The most impactful among us absorb blows of injustice and respond with love, proving that the light shines brightest in darkness when held with steady hands. By nurturing our inner light and engaging with the world thoughtfully, we can pave the way for a brighter, more compassionate future.

The Power of Self-Acceptance: Why Seeking Validation Is Like Chasing Shadows

Imagine life as a never-ending popularity contest where the rules keep changing. You might win some approvals, but you'll always find critics. Chasing validation from others is like trying to catch a shadow; no matter how fast you run, it's always out of reach. So why not skip the chase and find your own spotlight?

When you're comfortable with yourself, other people's opinions become background noise. You start moving to your own rhythm instead of matching someone else's beat. This self-confidence isn't just about being stubborn; it's about embracing your unique soundtrack and sticking to it, even when the crowd might not be cheering.

Let's be real: life can throw some serious curveballs. You'll stumble, faceplant, and get knocked down more than a few times. But here's the kicker: sometimes, the people who pick you up are strangers who surprise you with their kindness. Those unexpected allies can offer more genuine support than you might get from folks you thought were your "ride-or-die" crew.

Instead of judging others' flaws, how about we start some real conversations? We all have our struggles, and you'd be amazed at how many of us share the same battles when we drop the masks and talk openly. It's like finding a secret club where everyone gets each other's challenges.

Remember to keep checking in with your core values when you feel lost or stuck. Think of them as your GPS system guiding you back to what matters when you stray off course. Even in the darkest times, that inner light is like a torch, showing you through the fog.

Building solid relationships means letting go of snap judgments. Everyone's a work in progress, and so are you. Embrace imperfections, yours and theirs. Society pushes us into neat boxes, but real life is about the messy middle. True wisdom doesn't come from fitting perfectly into those boxes but dancing in the chaos.

Bruce Lee nailed it with his advice to "be like water." Water adapts to its container, flows around obstacles, and is gentle and powerful. When you let go of rigid ideas and stay open to new experiences, you become more adaptable, like water. Fresh opportunities and connections will flow if you let yourself be flexible.

Love is the secret ingredient for growth and connection. When you radiate self-love and compassion, you draw in people who vibe with that energy. Even when things don't go as planned, self-love keeps you steady until you find your tribe.

Life is a journey of constant self-discovery and evolving relationships. The more you stay true to yourself, the more you open up to new possibilities. Each day is a chance to embrace your inner water, flowing, adapting, and growing.

Sometimes, relationships may not keep up with your personal growth. It's tough but remember: aligning with your true self makes space for new, enriching connections. Your thoughts shape your reality, so practising self-love is essential for attracting the right people and opportunities.

Just like our bodies need good food to thrive, our minds and spirits need nourishing thoughts and positive environments. Think of it as feeding your whole self junk food. Negativity is like fast food for the soul, while healthy habits are gourmet for the heart and mind.

We all filter information that shapes our views. Some prefer comforting lies, but facing uncomfortable truths is what strengthens us. Be patient and empathetic when engaging with different perspectives. Encouraging growth through questions rather than demands helps foster a more understanding and inclusive world.

We all seek attention to some extent, whether to share knowledge, connect with others, or just be seen. The key is ensuring this desire aligns with your highest values and contributes positively. Be true to yourself, and remember: knowing and loving yourself first is crucial before handling others' judgments and validations.

So, let's ditch the endless chase for approval and focus on being our most authentic selves. By embracing self-acceptance, compassionate communication, and personal growth, we can confidently and joyfully navigate life's complexities.

> "The greatest recognition comes not from the applause of others but from the quiet confidence of knowing you've stayed true to yourself." – ***Steve Maraboli***

This quote emphasizes that real validation and satisfaction come from within, not from others' approval or praise. It means that true self-worth comes from being authentic and genuine to your values rather than seeking validation from others. "Quiet confidence" is about understanding and accepting yourself deeply, which offers a lasting sense of fulfilment compared to temporary applause or praise from others. While external approval can be short-lived, the confidence that comes from being true to yourself is much more enduring and meaningful.

11

Family Skeletons and Broken Mirrors: A Dark Comedy on Inherited Pain

Focus:

This chapter tackles generational trauma and the dark humour linked to inherited dysfunction. It reveals the lasting effects of abuse, neglect, and cultural silence through personal stories and social commentary. Trauma often becomes a family legacy, passed down and normalized until questioned. The chapter urges us to break this cycle through confrontation and healing, highlighting that facing our past is essential for freeing future generations.

Transmissions From Earth Realm:

- *"Some families pass down recipes. Mine passed down rage, silence, and a fear of vulnerability."*
- *"Generational trauma isn't always visible. It echoes in the arguments we avoid, the love we withhold, and the pain we*

normalize."

- *"When chaos is your comfort zone, peace can feel like danger."*
- *"We inherited dysfunction like furniture. Heavy, outdated, but too familiar to throw away."*
- *"He wasn't born a monster. He was made by a world that taught him pain was power."*
- *"Healing begins the moment we stop pretending the past didn't happen."*
- *"We don't just carry our ancestors' pain. We carry their silence, too."*
- *"Breaking the cycle means becoming the person you needed when you were a child."*

Did you know?

1. **Echoes of Childhood Trauma:** Individuals who experience abuse or severe neglect in childhood often struggle with severe difficulties in emotional regulation and self-worth. This unresolved trauma can manifest as chronic self-sabotaging behaviours, which perpetuate feelings of inadequacy and hopelessness throughout their lives.
2. **Mimicking Abuse Patterns:** Research shows that individuals who grew up in abusive environments are more likely to mimic those abusive patterns in their own relationships. This perpetuation of harm can create a cycle where each generation teaches the next to replicate the dysfunctional behaviours they experienced.
3. **Hypervigilance and Trust Issues:** Survivors of trauma

often develop a heightened state of hypervigilance, where they are excessively alert and anxious about potential threats. This constant state of readiness can make it nearly impossible for them to trust others, leading to isolation and difficulty in forming stable, healthy relationships.

4. **Unhealthy Coping Mechanisms:** Many hurt people resort to harmful coping mechanisms such as substance abuse, self-harm, or risky behaviours to manage their emotional pain. These methods often provide only temporary relief and can exacerbate their problems, creating a dangerous cycle of addiction and self-destruction.
5. **Trauma's Biological Impact:** Trauma can cause long-term changes in the brain's structure and function. For instance, prolonged exposure to stress hormones like cortisol can impair memory and learning, heighten susceptibility to mental health disorders, and alter the brain's stress-response systems, making it harder for survivors to cope with everyday challenges.

> *"Hurt people hurt people. But healed people heal people."*
> - ***From the Author.***

Family Feuds and Fists: A Dark Comedy on Dysfunction

When it comes to relationships, especially those built within families, talking about dysfunction is like peeling back layers of an onion. You never know which layer will make you cry the hardest. But as uncomfortable as it is, some truths must be aired out, even if that means dragging family skeletons into the light. In my case, reflecting on my own family's journey of trauma and survival feels both profoundly personal and eerily universal. There's an unspoken truth: hurt people often hurt others. The question is, where do we draw the line, and how do we break the cycle?

Take my maternal Grandad. By day, he was a hard-working man, the kind you'd find in any community sweating it out to provide for his family. But by night, the story shifted from provider to punisher. I wasn't alive during his worst days, but the stories paint a grim picture: a man so weighed down by life that his only release was through alcohol and violence. He became the monster he had probably been running from his whole life. There's something tragically poetic about the oppressed becoming the oppressor, hurt turning inward until it lashes out at everyone around it. He would come home after long days of hard labour in the racist, hostile environment of 1950s England. As a Jamaican immigrant, he was treated like dirt outside the house, but inside... inside, he made sure he was in charge at the expense of his family.

My Grandma, though she's a different story. She was the backbone, the one who held everything together. She was raising nine kids in a new country, and if that wasn't hard enough, she was doing it while facing violence from her husband. She was strong, no doubt about it, but that kind of strength comes with a heavy cost. And to think, back then, it was just something you dealt with. There were no shelters and no support networks. You couldn't call up a friend and say, "Hey, my husband's beating the hell out of me. Can I crash on your couch?" It just wasn't done. She had no choice but to stay, to keep going. Her strength wasn't celebrated; it was expected, even in silence.

You see, back then, abuse wasn't just tolerated. It was *ignored*. People didn't talk about what happened behind closed doors, and the idea of seeking help felt like betrayal. For black families especially, still establishing a sense of community in a new, often hostile country, you couldn't show weakness. Your opportunities were scarce, and even those came with a price. So, you endured. You swallowed the pain, gritted your teeth, and carried on.

But here's what haunts me: the idea that the provider, who's supposed to protect, becomes the most significant threat. It's like a sick joke. He was supposed to make things better, but instead, he made things so much worse. And the sad truth is, his actions weren't just born out of cruelty. They came from his own scars, the unresolved pain that shaped him long before he ever had a family of his own. I think about that a lot: the hurt he carried and passed on. Hurt doesn't just stay put. It spreads like a disease unless it's dealt with head-on.

This is the part that hits home: abuse isn't just about bruises or broken bones. It seeps into your very being, leaving marks you carry for life. My family has seen this firsthand. The trauma was passed down like some twisted inheritance, bleeding into relationships, into how we express love, into the way we deal with conflict. It's like encoded in your DNA, a constant battle between what you know and want to be.

But here's the thing: I'm proud to say a lot of my family decided not to let that trauma define us. It wasn't easy, and it wasn't always pretty. There were moments when the cycle nearly repeated itself. But resilience runs deep. It's not about pretending everything's fine or ignoring the pain. It's about facing it, acknowledging where it came from, and finding a way to break free from it. Our journey was difficult, but it was a journey we took together, and it's a journey that's possible for anyone who is willing to face their pain and work towards healing.

Some of us were saved by the hard lessons and the people who stepped in when the system failed. We didn't get here on our own. It took therapy, support, and a real commitment to breaking the cycle. There were moments of reckoning, sometimes painful, sometimes liberating, but each step brought us closer to healing. The idea that "hurt people hurt people" is true, but it doesn't have to stay that way. With the proper support and a commitment to healing, it is possible to break free from the cycle of trauma.

In the end, my family's story is one of both trauma and resilience. We've seen the worst of what unchecked pain can do but also learned how to build something better. The scars are still there, but they don't control us. By shedding light on the dark, twisted dynamics of abuse and trauma, we take away its power. And maybe, just maybe, we start the process of healing.

The Ghosts We Inherit: A Dark Comedy of Unresolved Trauma

Unresolved trauma is like an unwanted family heirloom passed down through generations, whether you want it or not, only instead of grandma's old brooch, it's a crippling emotional burden that no one really asked for. And yet, here it is, unpacked neatly into your life, delivered courtesy of your parents' unresolved childhood nightmares. It's fascinating (and tragic) how trauma gets transmitted across generations, as if the dysfunction is coded into your DNA, waiting for just the right moment to wreak havoc. My family? We've seen more than our fair share of it, and boy, do the patterns run deep.

Growing up in a family where dysfunction was as common as Sunday dinner, I learned early on that hurt people unintentionally and, of course, hurt others. It's not like anyone wakes up and says, "I think I'll emotionally scar my kids today." But the problem is, when you've never been shown how to cope with your own hurt, you have no idea how to avoid passing it on. My own family had more unspoken rules than a secret society. The worst rule? That trauma was just something you lived with. It never got talked about, never got dealt with. It was like the furniture in the house: always there, part of the scenery, impossible to ignore but never quite addressed.

Take my parents, for example. Like clockwork, they played out the same dysfunctional dynamics they saw growing up. Yelling to resolve conflict? Check. Emotional shutdowns instead of communication? Check. If you saw dishonesty and control growing up, you tend to model those same toxic behaviours as an adult. It's not like you consciously repeat the same patterns, but when chaos is all you've known, it feels like home.

I remember realizing at some point that I was falling into those same traps. I could see the patterns in my relationships, like reruns of a bad sitcom. Raised on a diet of dysfunction, I was mimicking behaviours without even thinking. It's funny, well, more tragic than funny, how what we're raised with becomes our norm, even if it's toxic. That's your relationship template when you grow up watching your parents solve problems by yelling or shutting down. Communication? Compromise? Setting boundaries? Those concepts might as well be in a foreign language.

Adults tend to cling to what's familiar, even when it's unhealthy. And that's how the cycle repeats. I've seen it play out in my family over and over again. My uncles, aunts, and cousins, all of us unintentionally carrying forward the trauma we never signed up for. It's like watching the same painful drama unfold at every family gathering with different faces and the same unresolved issues. There's no laugh track, just the silent understanding that we're all stuck in the same script, hoping someone will rewrite it.

Let's talk about the science behind it because here's where it gets darkly fascinating: trauma doesn't just affect you emotionally. It literally rewires your brain and alters your biology. That's right, the ghosts of past trauma embed themselves in your genes. Science calls it epigenetics, but I call it cosmic cruelty. Imagine this: your ancestors lived through trauma, and now your DNA is just waiting to unleash that trauma on you. Thanks, genetics! Studies have shown that childhood trauma can mess with the way your genes regulate stress hormones like cortisol. So not only are you dealing with the emotional baggage, but your body is primed to freak out at the slightest hint of stress, too. Lucky you.

And it doesn't stop there. These epigenetic changes get passed on, too. So your kids and their kids are all carrying the weight of trauma they never even experienced. I look at my family, and it's like we've all been handed a baton in a relay race we never wanted to run. Generations of unresolved trauma, wrapped up neatly and passed down as our inheritance.

In my family, I've seen firsthand how these emotional and biological scars play out. It starts with small things, like a family member's tendency to overreact to stress or get defensive at the slightest critique. But over time, those coping mechanisms wear thin. Anxiety becomes a constant companion. Depression creeps in. Some turn to alcohol or other unhealthy habits to numb the pain. Others just shut down emotionally, unable to process feelings because they never learned how.

Trauma doesn't just disappear because you ignore it. It festers, bubbling beneath the surface until it all spills out one day. And when it does, the damage is catastrophic. It manifests in panic attacks, rage, addiction, or worse. I've seen family members explode out of nowhere, and it's always the same story: years of unresolved trauma finally breaking through. That's the insidious thing about trauma: it never really goes away. You can push it down, suppress it, but eventually, it'll find a way out.

What's really messed up is how normal it becomes. You grow up in chaos, so you expect chaos. When things are calm, you almost don't trust it. If you're not yelling, something must be wrong. If you're not in control, you feel vulnerable. And if you've been taught that vulnerability leads to pain, you'll do anything to avoid it. Even if that means repeating the cycle of hurt. That's how generational trauma works. It's a self-perpetuating loop, playing out over and over again.

The only way to break the cycle is through self-awareness and hard work. Therapy, healthy relationships, and boundaries aren't just buzzwords. They're survival tools. It takes a conscious decision to say, "Enough. The trauma stops here." And even then, it's an uphill battle. I've seen some of my family members break the cycle, and it's nothing short of heroic. Make no mistake: breaking free of generational trauma isn't easy. It's messy, it's painful, and sometimes it feels impossible. But it's the only way forward.

In the end, the story of unresolved trauma isn't just my family's story it's a universal one. We all carry the ghosts of those who came before us, whether we realize it or not. But we also have the power to break free. It starts with acknowledging the past and ends with choosing a different future.

What else contributes to childhood trauma?

Our society has a way of wrapping violence in a pretty package, making it look acceptable or even heroic. Think about it: how many movies and TV shows glorify revenge and make it seem like getting even is justified and cool? Mix that with the normalization of corporal punishment at home, and you have a culture that teaches kids early on that hurting others is just how you handle your own pain. It's almost like we've handed out a playbook for perpetuating cycles of harm, where being hurt means you get a free pass to hurt someone else.

Then there's the "pick yourself up by the bootstraps" mentality, which makes things worse. Instead of addressing the fundamental, systemic issues that cause trauma, like poverty, discrimination, and lack of access to basic resources, society often blames the victim. "Why didn't you just leave?" becomes the question instead of "Why wasn't help available?" We enable toxic dynamics by placing the responsibility entirely on individuals while ignoring the structures that keep them trapped.

The reality is that poverty doesn't just make life complicated. It causes a constant state of toxic stress that weighs on families like a heavy cloud. It leads to parental mental health issues, substance abuse, domestic violence, and child neglect, with no real lifeline to pull them out. Discrimination plays a significant role, too, constantly reminding minorities that they're not safe, creating trauma responses like anxiety and hypervigilance that stick with you for life. Add in the lack of opportunity in underserved areas, and it's no surprise that cycles of dysfunction continue.

It's almost like trauma embeds itself in your very DNA. Stress changes your body chemistry, chronic inflammation, neural rewiring, and hormone imbalances—resulting in poor physical and emotional health. This is how the body tells the story of trauma when no other outlet is available.

The bottom line is that systemic inequity leaves families and communities without the support they need to break free. Add in the stigma surrounding mental health, and you've got generations of unresolved trauma, kept in the dark, waiting to erupt.

The Invisible Web of History: Black-on-Black Crime

When we talk about cycles of abuse, trauma, and dysfunction in our communities, it's impossible not to address the elephant in the room: **Black-on-Black crime**. This term gets thrown around in media as though it's some sort of inherent flaw within Black people, but let's not kid ourselves. This isn't about skin colour; it's about **systemic oppression**, **government neglect**, and the intentional manipulation of the environment we were forced into.

Let's be real. The crime in our communities is the byproduct of centuries of exploitation and marginalization. It's what happens when you stuff a group of people into underfunded neighbourhoods, cut off access to proper education, jobs, and mental health resources, and create policies that quite literally choke the life out of any potential growth. The term "Black-on-Black crime" doesn't even acknowledge the root of the issue. It simply shifts the blame inward, like it's our own doing.

But let's unpack that. How do you expect people to thrive when the system around them is designed to **divide and con-**

quer? From the days of redlining to today's mass incarceration practices, these policies were never about safety or improvement. They were about control. The government knew exactly what it was doing when it waged a so-called "war on drugs" in the '80s. Flood our neighbourhoods with crack, offer zero rehabilitation, and then conveniently label us as criminals. That's not accidental; that's intentional sabotage. It's trauma on a grand scale, playing out in our streets like a script someone else wrote.

When you create an environment where the **state** is your oppressor, where every opportunity feels like a mirage, and where desperation is normalized, you breed crime. It's the psychology of survival. Hurt people hurt people, but it's important to understand that **the hurt itself is often orchestrated**.

Calling it "Black-on-Black crime" without addressing the centuries of government policies, institutionalized racism, and intentional socio-economic isolation is not just lazy; it's complicit. It's like treating a wound but ignoring the knife still lodged in it. The violence we see today in Black communities is a direct reflection of a larger, historical violence inflicted upon us, systematically and relentlessly. And until we address that root cause, we'll just be stuck in this endless cycle, blaming ourselves for the trauma we didn't create but are forced to live out.

The Shocking Truth Behind Black-on-Black Crime: Systemic Betrayal and Generational Trauma

When we talk about Black-on-Black crime, we're not just discussing isolated incidents of violence; we're unravelling a grim saga of systemic failure and intentional neglect that has been baked into the very fabric of our society. The Kerner

Commission report, formed in the aftermath of the 1967 riots, revealed uncomfortable truths that still resonate today, exposing how generations of systemic racism and deprivation have fostered cycles of trauma and violence within Black communities.

The Kerner Commission did more than just scratch the surface. It delivered a brutal assessment of America's racial divide, laying bare that the riots were not random outbursts of chaos but the explosive result of long-standing, systemic injustices. This wasn't about a few bad apples. It was a national scandal of epic proportions. The Commission's report boldly stated that the riots were fueled by "deep-seated grievances" and "a climate of frustration and hopelessness" created by an uncaring system. Essentially, it revealed how systemic racism and economic neglect had transformed Black communities into battlegrounds of despair.

Imagine growing up in an environment where every chance to succeed is systematically stripped away. Schools are under-funded, job opportunities are scarce, and neighbourhoods are neglected. This is not a dystopian fiction but a harsh reality for many Black families. The Kerner Commission's findings showed that such environments were deliberately constructed and maintained by policies that prioritized the comfort of the privileged over the well-being of the oppressed. The result? A powder keg of frustration and anger that inevitably ignites into violence.

Consider the following: when children are raised in high-crime, high-poverty areas, the trauma they experience isn't just an unfortunate side effect. It's a predictable outcome of systemic neglect. The Commission's report emphasized that these environments were products of deliberate policy choices, not random misfortunes. These children are marinated in a culture of violence and instability, where survival often means adopting the very behaviours they see around them. This isn't just a personal failing but a direct result of the environments deliberately shaped by decades of discriminatory policies.

And here's where it gets even more disturbing: the trauma experienced in these communities doesn't just fade away. It's encoded into the very biology of the people living there. The Kerner Commission's findings align with modern epigenetic research, showing that trauma can be passed down through generations, altering how future generations react to stress and adversity. Essentially, the suffering of today's Black communities is a direct inheritance of systemic oppression, a cycle of trauma that the system has perpetuated and maintained.

The Commission's report called for urgent reforms to address these systemic failures, yet the changes have been slow and inadequate. The policies that allowed these conditions to flourish continue to stifle real progress. The result is a continued cycle of dysfunction, where systemic neglect breeds the very violence it purports to condemn.

Understanding this, it becomes glaringly evident that addressing Black-on-Black crime requires confronting the systemic injustices that have long been accepted as part of the status quo. We're not talking about minor tweaks to the system but a fundamental overhaul of policies that have systematically perpetuated racial and economic disparities. The Kerner Commission's report was a wake-up call, a shocking revelation of how deeply entrenched these issues are, and a clarion call for real, substantive change.

Until we face these uncomfortable truths and demand the systemic changes necessary to dismantle the structures of oppression, the cycle of trauma and violence will continue unabated. The Kerner Commission didn't just highlight a problem. It exposed a national scandal that we're still grappling with today. Suppose we genuinely want to end the cycle of Black-on-Black crime and trauma. In that case, we need to confront the systemic betrayals that have caused it and work toward a future where such injustices are a distant memory.

How can we avoid cycles of abuse?

Breaking the cycle of abuse isn't a simple "just stop it" situation. If only it were that easy. The truth is that healing from generational trauma requires a lot more than good intentions. It starts with something fundamental: having at least one stable, caring adult relationship. For many, that might've been a grandparent, a teacher, or a neighbour. Having someone who consistently shows up for you provides a sense of security that starts building the foundation of resilience.

But let's be real: emotional regulation and therapy are crucial, too. Learning how to name and tame those feelings bottled up for years can make all the difference between repeating old patterns and creating new ones. Cognitive reframing, looking at things from a healthier angle, gives you the tools to start changing the story you've been handed. It's not just about surviving the trauma but making sense of it and releasing the weight so it doesn't crush you.

Another key ingredient? Community support. Whether it's a school counsellor, a coach, or a mentor, having alternative examples of healthy relationships can give you hope that things don't always have to stay broken. If you grew up in chaos, seeing how calm and functional other families are can be shocking, but it's also liberating. Naming the dysfunction, recognizing the patterns, and deciding which behaviours stop with you that's where the real power lies.

Self-efficacy plays a massive role, too - believing you can make different choices than the ones modelled for you. Education, enrichment, and skills-building give you the confidence to break out of the mould. And when things get tough, having positive support systems to lean on helps you weather the storms without reverting to old, toxic coping strategies. Spirituality or a sense of purpose can also help, whether faith, personal values, or a moral compass. When you have something bigger than your pain to guide you, it reinforces hope and resilience.

One thing we often overlook is the importance of leading with compassion. Hurtful behaviour usually comes from unhealed hurt. It's easy to judge or shame someone for their dysfunction, but it's much harder to pause and ask, "Where's this coming from?" Separating the person from their survival mechanisms doesn't excuse harmful actions but opens the door to healing. Listening without assumptions, offering support, and providing access to resources like therapy, mentorship, and support groups can help break down the barriers that prevent people from seeking help.

It's a balancing act of holding someone accountable while meeting them where they are with empathy. Sharing stories of recovery and resilience shows that change is possible. Promoting trauma-informed perspectives in schools, workplaces, and public services builds a culture of understanding instead of judgment. In the end, it's about leading with compassion rather than criticism. When we understand the roots of dysfunction and provide the tools for healing, we remove the need for hurting people to keep hurting others. It's not about erasing the past but transforming the future.

> **"The more we focus on improving the conditions in which people live, rather than blaming them for their plight, the more likely we are to break the cycle of despair and create a future where everyone has a chance to thrive."** — *Adapted from the Kerner Commission Report*

12

Lost Minds, Broken Beliefs: The Dark Clash Between Reality and Faith

Focus:

This chapter examines the collision between reality, belief, and mental sovereignty. It explores how systems of power, from religion to government to the media, shape our thoughts and manipulate our perceptions. It challenges us to ask whether we are truly free thinkers or products of engineered ideologies. As it peels back the layers of spiritual confusion, historical distortion, and psychological control, it calls us to reclaim our inner authority and liberate our minds from the illusions that keep us confined. This is a wake-up call to question, dismantle, and rebuild what we believe.

Transmissions From Earth Realm:

- *"You don't have to be in a graveyard to be dead. Some of us are just shells walking the earth."*
- *"You become what you believe, especially when what you believe was never yours to begin with."*
- *"Faith isn't the problem. It's the people who twist it into a weapon of control."*
- *"Religion taught me to fear a hell I was already living through."*
- *"If your beliefs demand obedience but kill your individuality, they're not sacred. They're cages."*
- *"A system designed to protect itself will always demonize those who question it."*
- *"When your mind is colonized, your soul becomes collateral."*
- *"The truth isn't hidden. It's buried beneath what you've been told to believe."*

> *"You Become What You Believe"* - ***From the Author.***

1. **Historical Deception:** Think about how history has been twisted to justify oppression. Remember how colonial powers used religion and racial superiority to subjugate entire nations? They didn't just conquer lands; they rewrote beliefs to ensure the oppressed stayed down and the powerful stayed up. It's a painful reminder that belief systems can be engineered to serve those who want to control and exploit. But with critical thinking, we can unravel these deceptions and empower ourselves to

challenge the status quo. **Built-in Bias:** Have you ever wondered why the scales of justice sometimes seem so uneven? It's because belief systems are often embedded with systemic biases. Consider how Jim Crow laws in the U.S. upheld racial segregation under the guise of legality and fairness. The system was designed to ensure the privileged stayed privileged while others were kept in their place. This is why questioning authority is a right and a necessity in our quest for a more just society. **Economic Manipulation:** Look at how economic beliefs have shaped our world. The idea of "trickle-down economics" was sold to lift everyone up. Still, it has enriched chiefly the wealthy while leaving the rest of us struggling. It's a stark example of how belief systems can be used to perpetuate inequality and economic exploitation.

2. **Cultural Brainwashing:** Ever feel like media and education are feeding you a selective version of reality? That's because they often serve the interests of those in power. Governments and institutions have a knack for controlling the narrative, downplaying their mistakes, and pushing agendas that benefit them, while the truth remains hidden in plain sight.
3. **Psychological Control:** Consider how some groups and ideologies can manipulate your mind. High-control groups, or cults, are masters at isolating individuals, controlling information, and applying psychological pressure. They make you doubt your perceptions and beliefs, leading you into a world where you follow their dictates without question, often with devastating consequences for your freedom and well-being.

> *"Belief systems are the scaffolding of power; they hold up the structure of control while the masses, oblivious, are held captive in its shadow."* – **From the Author.**

Disturbing thoughts are like pounds of weight that exhaust the mind.

Do you ever wonder what runs through a person's mind? I've seen the disconnect between reality and a person's rationality. You might quickly label it as insanity. They're physically operational, but it seems nobody is behind the controls. Swallowed by that sunken place, spiralling, feeling trapped in the walls of their mind. Their overactive thoughts run rampant, congested and toxic, keeping them preoccupied without productive action. Processing so much internal data, likely triggered by past trauma and repetitive behavioural patterns, feels like Groundhog Day: no change, no progress.

You don't always see the signs of a person when they're at their best. When they fall off the bandwagon, you might expect them to get back up and return stronger, taking lessons learned to heart. The truth is, some of us don't bounce back. It's almost as if we convince ourselves that we can't or this is it. We throw in the towel before the next round begins.

We become empty shells. Droopy eyes and sunken faces, as if our souls have been sucked from our earthly space suits. You don't have to be buried in a graveyard to be dead. You can walk among the living and merely exist as an empty vessel. What was once a talented and vibrant being can be extinguished and swept under the carpet like dissolved matter.

I've had friends who lost their minds, sinking deep like the Titanic, and others who joined cults, worshipping textbooks and basing their entire ideology on them. Why let the food consume you and become what you're shovelling, driven by a religious belief system? Many of us lack free, organic critical thinking to the point where we can't even engage in humane, diverse debates without reverting to the source of our creator. Not to blow anyone's trumpet, but aren't we the creators? We have the knowledge to learn, wisdom to gain, and tools to build a practical, forward-thinking global society. God's work can't mean separation, segregation, and superiority over those who don't follow your path, can it?

I don't want to challenge anyone's religious views. Still, I heard a statement that resonated deeply with me: "Religion is for those who fear hell, and spirituality is for those who have already been there!" I've been there more than once. I don't fear this so-called hell because I've discovered nothing to fear. If I were to argue here, my God would not send me to burn in an eternal fire if I don't repent and claim Jesus Christ as my saviour. What kind of nonsense is that!? My God doesn't come with brutal threats, emotional blackmail, judgmental scrutiny, or a popularity contest. My God is humane, compassionate, peaceful, a healer, and a do-gooder of the world. My God is you and me, navigating and graduating through this growing pain of a school. Why believe in anything else but yourself?

I was born alone, and I will die alone. What you do in this life, you owe to yourself not to waste time on distractions that do not concern you or serve you globally. We have a connected consciousness with each other; our energy fields are magnets attracting what we participate in like-minded people with a common worldly resolve. However, many cults, groups, gangs, and institutions do not vibrate on these higher frequencies of spirituality. They all share one thing in common: they lack completeness of individuality.

Religion can be viewed as a divide, an indoctrination that robs you of self, character, and value. However, many people need religion to gravitate to higher knowledge, discipline, and generosity, which may not be achieved without it. Whatever we put our minds to, we can become overachievers and still find a level of collective consciousness in spirituality. There's no right or wrong way of doing things, thanks to free will. But just be mindful not to get stuck or hooked on ideologies. We truly are the creators, and we can activate our God Selves and let miracles work through us!

Not to backtrack, but as a final note, consider the amount of historical and present bloodshed religion has caused and continues to cause. More than any World War! As I understood, most major religious ideologies and scriptures are derived from the Emerald Tablets. Man painted their self-interests within their marketed belief system for you to believe in. With followers comes great control and power over the masses after planting the seeds of the narrative, which is still open for interpretation and can be an endless discussion and debate. Another divide-and-conquer elusive proposition. After all, we all have a worship gene; once it is activated, it's nearly impossible to deactivate.

Just how wired up are we? Are we complete human beings on Earth or just a questionable percentage?

The Real Gatekeepers: How Power Structures Shape Our Beliefs

The media, the police, the judges, and the lawyers might seem like they're working for us, but they often play by their own rules. While mainstream outlets and traditional institutions might shape narratives to fit their agendas, independent media and grassroots voices usually provide a more trustworthy perspective. We're taught to trust these structures and to believe in their commitment to law and order. Still, a closer look reveals that they often act as gatekeepers of power, influencing what we see, hear, and believe. If you've been relying on these traditional sources, prepare for a reality check. Once you start questioning their narratives, it's hard to look back.

Think about it: when COVID hit, every news outlet ran the same story, day in and day out, pumping fear into your veins. It was like they were reading from a script, a well-coordinated orchestra designed to keep you locked in your house, glued to your screen, and swallowing every mandate and restriction without question. And let's be clear: dissenters weren't just silenced; they were demonized. If you questioned the narrative, you were ridiculed, branded as a conspiracy theorist, or worse. Why? Because they can't afford to lose control over the belief system they've built around you. And the police? They were just the enforcers, cracking down on anyone who stepped out of line, making sure the narrative stayed intact. Courts upheld these lockdowns, judges rubber-stamped the rules, and anyone caught challenging the system found themselves on the wrong side of the law.

It's all about control. They don't care about your health, your rights, or your freedom. The entire system works together, not for justice, but for power. And here's where it gets even darker: people are walking among us who are truly above the law. Politicians, business elites, and high-ranking officials face one set of rules. At the same time, the rest of us are left to fend for ourselves. The courts, the police, and the media protect these people because they are part of the same corrupt network.

Take the paedophile scandals involving politicians and judges. Yes, you read that right. Judges are sitting on the bench right now who've been accused of some of the most heinous crimes imaginable, and yet nothing happens. These aren't just rumours or conspiracy theories but real, documented cases. But how often do you see these stories plastered across the front pages of mainstream news? How often do you see these predators face real consequences? You don't. Because they protect each other. They use their influence to sweep it all under the rug, and the media, the supposed "watchdogs" of society, turn a blind eye.

This isn't just favouritism but systemic corruption, plain and simple. Judges, who should be the last line of defence for justice, are guilty of crimes they would sentence others to life for. Lawyers who defend them manipulate the legal system to ensure their crimes never see the light of day. Police, who are supposed to investigate and protect the vulnerable, turn a blind eye when it comes to those in power. These institutions, which we've been taught to trust, are rotten from the inside out. They know it and use every tool ao maintain the illusion that the system works for them.

Do you really think it's a coincidence that when a high-profile figure is caught in a scandal, it quietly disappears? Celebrities, politicians, and judges facing accusations of sexual abuse, paedophilia, or corruption rarely face any real consequences.

They use the system to their advantage, such as plea deals, sealed records, and media silence. Meanwhile, the average person without money or connections faces the full wrath of the law for far less. People are rotting away in prisons because they can't afford a decent lawyer, trapped by a system designed to chew them up and spit them out. Public defenders? They're overworked, underfunded, and pressured to make deals rather than fight for their clients.

Do you want to talk about entrapment? The judicial system is nothing but a factory for turning poor defendants into prisoners. Prosecutors push plea deals with little regard for whether the person is guilty or innocent. The courts are a conveyor belt where justice takes a back seat to statistics and conviction rates. Those who can't afford a proper defence end up serving time, not because they're guilty, but because they're broke.

Meanwhile, those with power, whether it's a politician involved in a sex scandal, a CEO committing fraud, or a judge caught abusing children, walk away with nothing more than a slap on the wrist, if that. The people who are supposed to be protecting us are the very ones perpetrating the most vile acts, and the system lets them get away with it.

Let's be real: this isn't just corruption; it's a war on the truth. The system wants you to believe it's working in your favour while it protects the elite and feeds on the rest of us. The media, the courts, and the police don't serve justice. They serve power, and they've been doing it for a long time. What's more disturbing is that these scandals aren't exceptions; they're part of the system. And the more you look into it, the more you realize how deep the rot goes.

Ask yourself how many more scandals, cover-ups, and abuses

will happen before people wake up? The truth is right in front of us. They've created a belief system designed to keep us docile, obedient, and unaware of the real crimes happening behind closed doors. The media keeps feeding you the same narrative because they don't want you to see the cracks in the system. They want you to keep believing in the illusion of justice. But it's hard to ignore what's happening once you pull back the curtain.

The bottom line? We're living in a rigged system, and the people at the top are playing by a different set of rules. They protect, cover up each other's crimes, and keep the rest of us in the dark. The question is, how long will you keep believing their lies?

Trapped in a Broken System: Why We Keep Believing the Lies

This entire rigged system isn't just a power structure. It's a belief system. One that's been so deeply ingrained in us that we've worshipped it without even realizing it. Think about it: from a young age, we're taught to trust authority, respect the law, and believe that justice will always prevail. Yet time and again, we see countless victims, the wrongfully convicted, the marginalized, and those whose lives have been destroyed, not by their actions but by a system that was never designed to protect them.

And still, despite all the wake-up calls, we remain obedient. We follow the rules, pay our taxes, and do what we're told because we've been conditioned to believe in this system like it's some kind of holy truth. We don't question it because it's wrapped in law, order, morality, and justice. But what kind of justice lets the powerful prey on the weak, lets paedophiles and criminals walk free because of who they know or the position they hold? What type of system do we call fair when the guilty are protected and the innocent are silenced?

The sad reality is that we've been lulled into this false sense of security, tricked into believing that this system is infallible. We worship it because we've been taught to fear what happens if we don't. Step out of line, and you face consequences. But those at the top? They step out of line, and the system bends to accommodate them. The truth is that this belief system operates like any other; it relies on our faith, our blind trust, and our obedience to survive.

So, the real question is, why do we keep feeding into it? Why do we keep bowing to a system repeatedly showing that it doesn't care about us? It's not just the scandals, the cover-ups, the lies; it's the entire framework that holds us captive and keeps us from breaking free and demanding something better. We've had the wake-up calls, but we keep hitting snooze. It's time to recognize this belief system for what it is: a trap designed to keep us worshipping a broken order while those in control stay untouchable. Until we confront that, we'll remain obedient to a system that will never serve us.

From Slavery to Bailouts: How We're Still Paying the Price for the Elite's Exploitation

Let's get brutally honest: the elites in control today didn't just waltz into their positions of power. They clawed, connived, and manipulated their way to the top while leaving a trail of deceit and exploitation. And the proof? It's right in front of us if we dare to look.

Take the 2008 financial crisis as an absolute masterclass in the financial heist. Major financial institutions pushed toxic mortgage-backed securities onto unsuspecting investors and then bet against them. The resulting collapse didn't just shake the global economy; it triggered the biggest taxpayer-funded bailout in history. The U.S. government dished out over $700 billion to rescue the entities that caused the mess, roughly equivalent to $1 trillion today. The public footed the bill, while those responsible came out richer than ever. It's a textbook example of elites profiting from the chaos they created, leaving ordinary people to pick up the tab.

Now, let's rewind to a darker chapter of slavery. In Britain, when the transatlantic slave trade was abolished in 1807 and slavery itself in 1833, the British government didn't just end a monstrous system; they handed out a £20 million compensation package to slave owners. That amount, about £17 billion in today's money, was a taxpayer-funded payout for their so-called "loss of property." The actual victims, the freed individuals, got nothing but systemic racism and economic disenfranchisement. Imagine being forced to compensate your abuser for the end of their abusive relationship!

Across the Atlantic, when the U.S. abolished slavery in 1865, there was no compensation for slave owners. Still, the economic burden fell squarely on the newly freed individuals. They faced a mountain of systemic barriers while their former masters kept their wealth and power. It's as if the end of slavery didn't truly end the exploitation. It just shifted the burden onto those who had suffered the most.

Fast forward to today, and it's no surprise that many in power are the direct descendants of those slave owners. The great-great-grandchildren of people who amassed fortunes through blood, violence, and exploitation still benefit from inherited wealth, land, and influence. These elites have perpetuated their power through generations, leveraging their legacy of privilege to maintain control.

And here's the kicker: these elites who've built their empires on suffering set the rules. They control the media, the legal system, and the political institutions that are supposed to serve justice. Instead, these systems are used to preserve their dominance and manipulate the narrative to keep us in check.

The belief system we've been taught to trust is a well-oiled illusion meticulously designed to keep us obedient and unaware. It's a system built on a foundation of historical exploitation and contemporary deceit. The same bloodlines that thrived on oppression and manipulation are still pulling the strings today.

So, here's the hard truth: we're still being controlled by those who have perpetuated cycles of exploitation and injustice for generations. It's high time we wake up, confront this reality, and challenge the system rigged against us. We've been following orders from people who care only about maintaining their power at our expense. The time for questioning, reform, and rebellion is now.

13

Political Games and Hidden Aims

Focus:

This chapter exposes the carefully choreographed illusion of politics as we know it. It reveals how power is hoarded, not shared, and how public trust is weaponized to maintain control. From media manipulation and rigged systems to historical deception and systemic inequality, it shows that what we call democracy often serves the privileged few. By understanding the games being played and the hidden aims behind them, we can begin to reclaim the power that has always belonged to the people. Change starts with pulling back the curtain.

Transmissions From Earth Realm:

- *"Politics isn't broken. It was built this way."*
- *"We aren't disillusioned. We're finally seeing through the illusion."*
- *"You can't vote away a system designed to silence your voice."*

- *"Corruption doesn't hide anymore. It thrives in plain sight."*
- *"The people in power aren't failing. They're succeeding at protecting their interests."*
- *"Public distrust isn't a flaw. It's a tool they use to consolidate more power."*
- *"They give us elections to feel heard, but the decisions were made long before we cast our vote."*
- *"If truth is the threat, then maybe lies have always been the law."*

Did you know?

1. **Corruption Breeds Silence**: Political systems often perpetuate a culture of silence where whistleblowers and truth-tellers are silenced or punished. From rigged elections to backroom deals, those in power manipulate information, ensuring that corruption remains hidden beneath layers of deception.
2. **Weaponizing Ideology**: Governments and political elites frequently exploit ideologies, whether religious, nationalist, or cultural, to manipulate public opinion and justify oppressive policies. These ideologies are often wielded as weapons to maintain control and divide populations, a tactic that, once understood, can empower us to see through the manipulation. **Profiting from War**: The military-industrial complex thrives on global conflict. Political leaders and private corporations often benefit from war, ensuring that instability continues for economic

gain. At the same time, ordinary people bear the brunt of violence and destruction.

3. **Systematic Disempowerment**: Political structures are designed to keep the most vulnerable disempowered, maintaining an elite ruling class. Whether through voter suppression, media manipulation, or legal loopholes, political games serve to limit the voice and influence of marginalized communities.
4. **Public Distrust as a Tool**: Politicians sometimes deliberately foster public distrust in institutions to manipulate voters. By creating chaos and disillusionment, they can seize more power under the guise of "restoring order," all while undermining democratic processes.

> *"When will I finally get to rest through this oppression?*
> *They punish the people that's askin' questions*
> *And those that possess steal from the ones without possessions."*
> ***– 2Pac – Me Against the World***

Political Games and Hidden Aims

What if everything you thought you knew about politics was just one big Truman Show, minus the charm? What if the system designed to represent your interests was rigged from the start, with every move and decision choreographed behind the scenes? That's the unsettling reality: we find ourselves in a political game where the rules are set by those we never see, and the outcomes seem predetermined, no matter how much we're told otherwise.

As a citizen who used to follow politics closely, I believed that my vote mattered and that change was just one election away. However, the more I observed, the more it became clear: it's all a carefully crafted illusion. Every election cycle feels like reruns of the same show, with different characters and the same plotlines. Promises are made, hopes are raised, but when it's time for action, we're left with nothing but excuses and more of the same. We're stuck in a loop, endlessly replaying the same frustrations, while the real game happens behind closed doors. But we, as the public, have the power to change this narrative.

Politics is sold to us as a competition, a race where our voices and votes matter. But let's be honest; what we see is just the surface. The hidden agendas that drive the system are buried beneath layers of political theatre. The boardrooms, the lobbying firms, and the corporate money dictate the terms, not the will of the people. We're distracted by the noise of campaigns and media spectacles while the real decisions are made out of sight.

This chapter isn't just about critiquing the system. It's about pulling back the curtain. It's about understanding that what looks like a democratic process is often a performance meant to keep us engaged without giving us real power. Beneath the political games we watch on the surface are hidden aims that shape our lives in ways we rarely see until it's too late. By exposing these deeper forces, I hope we can begin to see the system for what it is and maybe even find ways to reclaim the power hidden from us all along. Understanding the system is the first step to reclaiming our power.

What is Politics?

Politics is, at its core, the art of governing a process that dictates how society is run. It's not just about governments, laws, and elections but about how power flows through every corner of society. In theory, it's a system of decision-making that should serve the people. Still, in practice, it often feels more like a battleground for competing interests. Politicians, voters, activists, and powerful lobbyists vie for influence, shaping policies on everything from the economy to healthcare and education. The ideologies we align with, whether liberalism, conservatism, or socialism, frame these debates, guiding who gets to wield power and how it's distributed.

Yet beneath this surface lies something darker: a game where hypocrisy and bias often rule the day. Those in power are rarely neutral, driven by party loyalty, special interests, and money. Politicians know how to manipulate public sentiment using contentious issues like immigration or welfare as tools to rally support, while often doing little to address the underlying problems. Media plays its role in this, selectively amplifying or downplaying stories to fit their agendas, keeping us divided and distracted from the real power structures at play.

So where does that leave us? Disillusioned, often. Scrolling through news feeds, it's clear that many of us are exhausted by the endless cycle of debates, scandals, and broken promises. It's easy to feel like the best response is to disconnect, step away from the noise of politics, and refocus on what actually matters in our lives. But while it's tempting to tune out, we can't afford to be completely absent from the political arena. The system may be flawed, but it still undeniably impacts our daily lives, and understanding this can help us stay engaged and connected.

At the heart of this divide is class. Politics doesn't just fail to serve the majority it actively favours the wealthy and well-connected. Policies are crafted to protect the interests of the rich. At the same time, the working class bears the brunt of unfair tax codes and economic policies that widen the gap between the haves and the have-nots. These inequalities go beyond wealth, bleeding into every facet of society, race, gender, and ethnicity, creating a hierarchy where some lives are valued more than others.

This isn't a new phenomenon. The political structures we navigate today are built on centuries of exploitation and violence, from the colonization of Indigenous lands to the modern-day disparities in wealth and opportunity. The history of atrocity informs the present, and challenging these systems is no small feat. But to move forward, we need to confront these uncomfortable truths. We must begin reimagining what society could look like if we stripped away the labels that divide us and focused on the collective good. This challenge can motivate us to change.

Imagine a world where we prioritized humanity over power and lived in true harmony with each other and the planet. This may sound like an impossible dream, but it offers a glimmer of hope and an invitation to think beyond the structures dividing us. Politics may be inescapable, but we can still work to reshape it in a way that serves us all, not just the privileged few.

Potential Solutions or Alternatives

It's easy to feel overwhelmed, like we're just cogs in a machine that's too broken to fix. But instead of just venting our frustrations, what if we started thinking about real change ways to make the system at least a little more bearable?

First, there's no question that political reform is long overdue. The way things are structured now, it's no surprise people feel disconnected and disillusioned. We need more transparency and accountability in politics. Imagine if politicians couldn't make empty promises without facing real consequences. What if every campaign promise had to be backed by a plan? And if they didn't follow through, there'd be consequences for the individual and their entire party. That would force them to think twice before spinning the same old rhetoric.

Then, there's the issue of engagement. People often feel like their voices don't matter; given the current system, it's hard to blame them. But what if we could shift that? What if we created more opportunities for meaningful participation? We need more than just a vote every few years. We need systems that allow us to keep politicians in check and ensure they listen, not just during election season. Maybe that looks like empowering local councils or creating online platforms where citizens can weigh in on the issues that affect them day-to-day.

Speaking of online platforms, grassroots movements are more critical now than ever. Social media can be both a curse and a gift, but it's a tool that has the power to organize and mobilize real change. It's time to stop waiting for politicians to fix things they won't. Actual change comes from the ground up, from people tired of the status quo and ready to fight for something better.

Lastly, we need to address political education. Most people go through life without fully understanding how the system works, and honestly, that's by design. But imagine if political literacy became a priority taught in schools and communities, ensuring that everyone understood their rights, knew how to organize, and held power accountable. It wouldn't happen overnight, but it's something we could work toward, slowly but surely.

In the end, complaining won't get us far. We must start reclaiming control and making the system work for us instead of against us. It won't be easy, but it's possible if we're willing to fight for it.

The Illusion of Power and Social Conditioning

At its core, absolute power has always rested with the people. Yet, we're led to believe otherwise through fear-mongering and social conditioning. One concept that comes to mind is the Dunning-Kruger Effect. Those with limited knowledge or skill tend to overestimate their abilities in this psychological phenomenon. At the same time, experts recognize the complexity and limitations of their understanding. On a larger scale, this bias plays out in how we perceive politics, media, and societal norms.

Think about how the media operates. The constant flood of sensationalized stories, violence, scandals, and disasters creates the illusion of a world in perpetual crisis. This is by design. The media, especially the 24-hour news cycle, keeps us in fear and distraction, diverting our attention from the deeper, more systemic issues. Immigration is a perfect example: news outlets frequently focus on isolated incidents, exaggerating threats and stoking unnecessary fear, which fosters division among the public.

We're also shaped by social conditioning from an early age. Educational systems and family structures often promote a narrow, one-sided view of history that aligns with the dominant political or cultural ideology. In many countries, history is taught from the perspective of the powerful, often excluding alternative narratives. Take colonial history: in the UK, textbooks might emphasize the so-called benefits of the British Empire, while in formerly colonized nations, the focus is on exploitation and resistance. These conflicting narratives highlight how history is skewed to serve those in power, ultimately shaping how we see ourselves and the world around us.

The cycle of power and manipulation extends beyond the media. It's a grand chess game where wealth and influence dictate the rules. If you don't have the right connections or financial backing, your chances of making an impact in politics are slim. The system is rigged: money leads to power, and that power is used to gain even more money, perpetuating a cycle of corruption.

A prime example of this is lobbying in the United States. Large corporations and special interest groups pour millions into lobbying efforts to sway legislation in their favour, often at the expense of the public. This distorts the very idea of democracy, as policies are crafted to protect corporate profits rather than the welfare of the people. This same dynamic is present in other nations, where political donations and behind-the-scenes influence further deepen inequality and injustice.

Meanwhile, the elites present themselves as paragons of virtue with polished appearances, carefully crafted speeches, and pristine public images. However, the reality of their actions often tells a different story, one of exploitation, greed, and manipulation. The contrast between their public personas and the grim reality of their decisions is as stark as the difference between a tailored suit and dirty laundry hidden away from sight.

To challenge this, we must demand systemic change. While "ethically cleansing" political and corporate leadership may sound extreme, it speaks to the urgent need for integrity, transparency, and accountability. It's not about literal cleansing; it's about transforming the system into one that genuinely serves the people it's supposed to represent.

By understanding the mechanisms of power and social conditioning and recognizing the corruption and manipulation that hold us back, we can reclaim our power and demand a system that truly works for all.

Reclaiming Power in a Flawed System

Feeling powerless in a corrupt political system is understandable, but that doesn't mean we're entirely out of options. Real change often starts with small actions from ordinary people. Here's why getting involved still matters, even when the odds seem stacked against us:

1. **Local Wins Matter**: Focusing on local issues can still lead to real improvements, even if the big picture looks grim. Fixing problems in our communities can make a tangible difference, from better schools to cleaner parks. Start small and see how these local wins can build momentum.
2. **Pressure for Change**: Grassroots actions can help chip away at the system. When people band together and push for reform, they can significantly impact the situation. It might take time, but history shows that pressure from below can eventually lead to substantial changes at the top.
3. **Building New Systems**: Sometimes, the best way to deal with a corrupt system is to create alternatives. By supporting local businesses, forming community groups, or backing independent media, we can build something

new that works better for us.

4. **Awareness and Advocacy**: By speaking out and staying informed, we raise awareness about corruption and the need for change. Educating others and highlighting issues can mobilize more people and help build a movement that holds power accountable.
5. **Personal Empowerment**: Taking action, no matter how small, gives us a sense of control and purpose. It helps us stay connected to our values. It reminds us that every bit of effort counts, even if the results aren't immediate.
6. **Culture of Accountability**: Persistent advocacy can gradually shift the political culture towards more transparency and accountability. Even if we can't fix everything overnight, our ongoing efforts can help foster a more honest and open system over time.

So, while the system might be flawed, getting involved and making a difference where we can is still worth it. Small actions can lead to significant changes, and staying engaged helps us fight for a better future.

14

The Injustice Within: My Story Inside and Out

Focus:

This chapter pulls back the curtain on justice, exposing the system's inner rot through lived experience on both sides of the prison bars. It challenges our notions of guilt, punishment, and authority, revealing a reality where truth is silenced, and power shields the guilty. We're invited to confront the illusion of justice, acknowledge the corruption hiding in plain sight, and recognize how collective silence fuels oppression. In the ruins of a broken system, a more profound truth emerges. Liberation begins when we no longer consent to the lies. The journey isn't just about prison; it's about waking up and understanding your role in challenging perceptions of justice and authority.

Transmissions From Earth Realm:

- *"The courtroom wasn't where justice was served. It was where my spirit was sentenced to silence."*
- *"Prison didn't confine me. It stripped away the noise so I could finally hear myself."*
- *"The real criminals wear suits and write laws, while the system cages those who refuse to kneel."*
- *"Justice isn't blind. It's willfully looking away when power is the accused."*
- *"I lost my mind only to gain something more dangerous to them: consciousness."*
- *"Being labelled a criminal was the price I paid for refusing to play their game."*
- *"Freedom didn't begin with release. It began the moment I stopped believing their version of truth."*
- *"This isn't just my story. It's the mirror we avoid, reflecting a world too afraid to face itself."*

Did I ever mention I experienced prison both as a convicted criminal and a member of staff? It's not the easiest subject to discuss, but I need to highlight how those experiences shaped my views on justice or the lack of it.

I'll start with this: I held my hands up to the unfortunate circumstances of possessing items that may or may not be illegal in the UK. Why do I say "may not be"? Because these items were never independently inspected, and no one challenged the evidence. What I was being tried for wasn't illegal in many other countries. A decade later, it's even clearer that what I possessed might not have been prohibited. My legal defence was laughable; I was silenced in the courtroom. Key character and witness statements were wrongfully withheld, and they concocted fabricated defences because I refused to cooperate. Threatened with an even harsher sentence, I changed my plea to guilty to avoid the heavier blow.

The corruption was laid bare before my eyes. The police, the lawyers, the judge, they were all in on it, working together to silence me. It wasn't about justice. It was about control. Who's going to believe a convicted criminal, right? They don't want the truth to see the light of day. This blatant injustice is what I want you to understand and empathize with.

The Real Prison

Let me tell you, from experience, that the system is corrupt. I've had lawyers, both in and out of prison, flat-out tell me, "There is no justice." We're fed this lie to keep us in line and control us. The real power lies with those at the top. They control the narrative, and we're too busy fighting each other to see the bigger picture.

We have criminals within the justice system sentencing so-called criminals. The ones creating the laws like Prince Edward, Tony Blair, and George Bush—get away with it all. They're protected by the very institutions meant to uphold justice. And we, the taxpayers, are complicit. We enforce these systems, but where is the justice? This is why we need to collaborate to demand change and restore justice.

So, let me ask you, who's really in jail? Looking around, I realized there wasn't much difference between the world outside and the prison I was in. We're all prisoners in this system. The police? The biggest gang in service to the overlords. And we're all complicit in the corruption while they steal our resources and control our minds.

My Rude Awakening

I was devastated. Thrown into a pit of insanity and harassment that went on for over a year while on police bail. It was a calculated attack on my mental health. I used to say the world is crazy, except for me. After everything, that still feels true today. But maybe I did lose my mind, or rather, I was forced to wake up in a way that felt like shock therapy.

Every day I spent in prison, I didn't feel guilt for the so-called crimes they pinned on me. In fact, in that confinement, away from the circus of lies and manipulation, I felt a strange sense of freedom. Clarity. It was as if, being away from the noise of society, I finally found some peace. Ironically, the courtroom is where I truly died, silenced, voiceless, in a place that decided my fate but wouldn't even listen to me. I felt like a ghost in my own body. My spirit was left in that courtroom, killed by the system.

Still, I had hope in appealing the judge's decision and in the love and support of my friends and family.

Losing My Mind to Gain Consciousness

In that cell, stripped of all my material possessions and the distractions of everyday life, I found myself at a crossroads. It was strange, physically confined, yet mentally free. No more noise or chaos; I started to rewrite my life's blueprint. Maybe this was the wake-up call I needed.

What is our purpose? Why do we experience both love and pain, life and death? In the solitude of that prison, I faced my biggest fear: being locked up. But as I confronted it, I realized it was just another illusion, like many things in life.

Each day in that quiet space pushed me to dig deeper. I began to see my fears for what they were: constructs created by society, not truths I had to live by. I learned that pain isn't just something to endure; it can be an influential teacher. It guides us to understand ourselves better and helps us find our place in the world.

As I accepted my past and the choices that brought me here, I embraced the duality of life, the joy and the sorrow as essential parts of the human experience. I discovered that consciousness isn't just about being awake; it's about recognizing how our inner selves connect with the world around us.

Prison became an unexpected sanctuary where I could silence the outside world and listen to myself. In that stark environment, I found freedom in letting go of outdated beliefs and unexamined fears. I realized that the real prison wasn't the cell; it was the limitations I had put on my own mind.

Losing my mind was actually the key to gaining consciousness. I found clarity, resilience, and a sense of purpose. Awakening isn't a one-time event; it's a journey. Each moment challenges us to question our assumptions and embrace the complexity of life. Through my experience, I learned that every struggle holds the potential for growth and understanding, guiding us toward who we are meant to be. This personal growth is what I want to inspire in you.

Enlightenment in Confinement

Here's the thing: I didn't really suffer in prison. Sure, there were emotional adjustments, but I wasn't meant to be there, at least not for punishment but for enlightenment. It was a break from the outside world's noise, a chance to look within and wake up.

I had a guiding voice, motivating and pushing me forward. The prison wasn't time wasted. I learned I connected, and

I listened to the stories of others, some of whom, like me, didn't belong there. The prison wasn't filled with "lowlifes" or "scumbags", as you might think. I met lawyers, doctors, counsellors, and even entrepreneurs. People from all walks of life.

The class system doesn't exist behind bars, although sentencing does differ between race and background. And what do you notice? The 1%, the ones in power who make the laws, never face the consequences. You see scandals in the media, but what happens? Nothing. This stark reality made me question the very nature of justice and the flawed system we all live in.

Unmasking the Protectors: A Web of Corruption and Silence

The institutions designed to uphold justice often shelter the worst offenders, creating a chilling reality where those in power are shielded from accountability. This isn't just a hypothetical scenario. It's a pervasive issue entrenched in our society, with far-reaching consequences.

Take the case of Jimmy Savile, a media icon whose decades-long reign of abuse was enabled by a network of complicity within the BBC and law enforcement. Despite numerous allegations, Savile evaded justice until his death, leaving behind a legacy of trauma for his victims. Similarly, the Stephen Lawrence case unveiled systemic failures within the police force. Lawrence, a Black teenager, was murdered in a racially motivated attack in 1993. Still, the initial police investigation was marred by incompetence and prejudice. It took years of campaigning from his family and activists to expose the cover-up and demand accountability, highlighting how institutions protect their own while failing the vulnerable.

Derek Chauvin, the former police officer who murdered

George Floyd, became a symbol of systemic racism within law enforcement. Despite the overwhelming evidence against him, Chauvin's actions were enabled by a culture prioritizing protection over justice, sparking global outrage and protests. Then there's Wayne Couzens, the Metropolitan Police officer who murdered Sarah Everard. His position granted him an authority that he abused horrifically, revealing how those tasked with protecting the public can become predators instead. Couzens was a trusted officer, yet he exploited that trust, again exposing the failings within the police to safeguard those they serve.

The BBC has also found itself embroiled in controversy with figures like presenter Huw Edwards, illustrating the broader issue of accountability in media and politics. When public figures wield influence, the lines between justice and cover-up can blur alarmingly.

Even the highest echelons of society have not escaped scrutiny. Figures like Prince Andrew have been accused of heinous acts yet often evade the consequences due to their status and connections. The protection these individuals receive is part of a broader narrative where power shields the guilty, leaving the vulnerable unprotected.

In the backdrop of this troubling narrative lies a big political cover-up that stretches back decades. A dossier prepared over 30 years ago by a determined member of Parliament warned of a powerful paedophile ring involving "big, big names." Yet, the silence and inaction that followed demonstrate how deeply entrenched these protective mechanisms are within our institutions.

The Verdict

We live in a world run by white-collar criminals, and we blindly trust them to deliver justice. We judge convicts, but we're the ones trapped in this corrupt system. The next time you look at a former convict with disgust, remember you're a part of this, too.

It's time to wake up. I rest my case, but this conversation doesn't end here. Real change requires collective action, starting with seeing through the lies. We've been duped, controlled, manipulated. It's time to break free.

Because if we don't fight for ourselves, who will?

The Final Verdict: Breaking the Chains of Silence

As I reflect on my journey through the corridors of power and deception, I am struck by a sobering truth: We are all actors in a play written by those who have long since abandoned the script of justice. We wear our roles of prisoner, officer, victim, and witness like masks, each hiding a deeper reality. But beneath this façade lies a choice: to remain complicit in the silence or to rise against it.

We are often led to believe that justice is a privilege reserved for the righteous and the innocent, but what happens when the very systems designed to protect us are the ones that enslave us? We must ask ourselves: how long will we allow the powerful to manipulate the narrative. At the same time, the rest of us languish in the shadows?

This isn't just my story; it's a collective narrative of betrayal that resonates through countless individuals silenced by fear, stigma, and ignorance. Like a thread, each story weaves into the fabric of a society that has forgotten its moral compass. Ignoring the truths of those who have walked through the fire, we risk burning in our own complacency.

But the good news? We have the power to rewrite this narrative. We can choose to challenge the status quo, dismantle the structures that perpetuate injustice, and amplify the voices that have long been hushed. Our strength lies not in our individual battles but in our collective resolve to hold the powerful accountable and reclaim our humanity.

So, let us cast aside the shackles of silence and fear and confront the uncomfortable truths that lurk beneath the surface. In the end, the real prison isn't made of concrete and bars; the invisible chains of complicity and apathy bind us.

It's time to rise, to speak, to act. The world is watching, and change is possible if we dare to envision a future free from the corruption that has held us captive for far too long.

Let this be our rallying cry: we will no longer be prisoners of a broken system. Together, we will forge a path toward justice, one voice, one story, and one truth at a time.

15

The Most Important Stories You're Not Hearing About and Why You Should Care

Focus:

This chapter is a wake-up call. It shines light on the stories buried under distraction and noise that shape your future. From environmental collapse and digital surveillance to rising inequality and dying democracies, the issues we ignore today will define the world our children inherit. This isn't a distant crisis. It's a present one. The madness of the modern world isn't accidental; it's systemic. But by paying attention, we reclaim the moment we start to change when change becomes possible. This is a call to consciousness.

Transmissions From Earth Realm:

- *"The planet isn't dying. It's being killed, and the killers are in power while we scroll past the crime."*
- *"We drown in entertainment while the air we breathe grows toxic. Distraction is the new addiction."*
- *"Mass surveillance is the digital cage we built ourselves, pixel by pixel, in the name of convenience."*
- *"The billionaires aren't winning. They're rigging the game while convincing us it's fair."*
- *"Social media doesn't just steal our time. It hijacks our minds and sells the pieces to the highest bidder."*
- *"Your silence is someone else's profit. Your attention is their currency."*
- *"The systems are broken by design. If you feel powerless, that was always part of the plan."*
- *"The future isn't written yet, but our window to hold the pen is closing fast."*

The world is changing in ways that directly affect your life, family, and future. Yet, many of these urgent issues are flying under the radar, buried by more immediate distractions.

Here's what's happening and why you must pay attention...

> By 2050, more plastic will be in the oceans than fish by weight. Microplastics have been found in human blood, lungs, and placentas, a toxic legacy of unchecked consumerism. More than 1 million species face extinction. The Amazon, often called the

> lungs of the Earth, now emits more carbon than it absorbs due to relentless deforestation. These are not warnings from a distant future. They are the headlines of now. The Earth is not dying naturally; it's being poisoned, burned, and exploited by design. And as the ecosystems collapse, so do the systems meant to sustain our freedom, sanity, and survival.

In ***Earth Realm - Home of the Mentally Ill,*** humanity stands as a species on the brink, brilliant in its capacity for innovation, yet deeply fractured in its relationship with nature, each other, and its own sanity. The book's title isn't merely a metaphor; it's a mirror reflecting the unsettling truth that we, as a collective society, suffer from mass psychosis, one where greed, power, and control overshadow the most basic principles of survival and cooperation.

The world around us is changing in ways that will directly affect your life, family, and humanity's future. But many urgent, existential issues are being overshadowed by distractions, whether political squabbles, endless entertainment, or the constant barrage of consumerism. Beneath this noise lie the real stories: the ones that reveal a planet teetering on the edge of collapse, a society plagued by inequality, and a world where technology has advanced faster than our moral frameworks.

The question posed by ***Earth Realm - Home of the Mentally Ill*** is not just "What's happening?" It's **why we aren't doing anything about it.** Why are we so blind to our self-destruction, so disconnected from the urgency of the moment? These aren't distant, abstract problems; they are real, present threats shaping the world you live in. They are poisoning the air you breathe, eroding your freedoms, and paving the way for an unstable future for your children.

This book confronts the uncomfortable truth that our failure to act is rooted not in ignorance but in a collective mental and moral decline. Yet, though time is running out, there is still time to awaken from this stupor, recognize what is at stake, and take responsibility for the future of our species and our planet.

Here are the most pressing issues humanity faces, the ones most of us are ignoring and why you should care deeply about every single one of them.

1. Your Planet is Dying, and It's Taking Your Future with It

Why It Matters: Imagine a world where food shortages are the norm, species disappear before your children can even know they exist, and pollution affects everything you eat and drink. This is happening *right now*.

- **Deforestation**: The Amazon, often called the "lungs of the Earth," is being cut down at an alarming rate. Without it, the air you breathe becomes dirtier, and the balance of the global climate crumbles.
- **Plastic Pollution**: Every day, the plastic you throw away finds its way into oceans, poisoning marine life. Worse still, microplastics end up in your body, yes, inside *you,* with unknown long-term health risks.

Why You Should Care: If we don't take drastic action, the environment that sustains us will no longer be able to. This isn't just about saving the planet; it's about saving *ourselves.*

2. Your Data Is Being Stolen, Sold, and Weaponized

Why It Matters: Every time you log onto social media or search for something online, your personal information is often collected and sold without your consent. But it's more sinister than just targeted ads.

- **Surveillance Everywhere**: Governments and corporations track everything from your face to your online activity. Facial recognition is already used to suppress dissent in some countries, and it's spreading fast.
- **Invasive Technologies**: Smart home devices are collecting more information than you think. That voice assistant you use? It's always listening.

Why You Should Care: Your privacy is being stripped away bit by bit, and once it's gone, it's almost impossible to get back. This is not a reversible process; it's gone once your privacy is compromised. You deserve to live without being watched every second of the day, and we need to act now to protect our privacy.

3. The Rich Are Getting Richer, and You're Paying for It

Why It Matters: While you're working harder than ever, the wealthiest 1% are consolidating power. This isn't just about billionaires buying yachts. It's about them shaping laws that benefit themselves at the cost of the rest of us.

- **Corporate Control**: Mega-corporations influence government policies on taxes, healthcare, and workers' rights, making it harder for ordinary people to get ahead.
- **Rigged System**: Wealth inequality is growing so extreme that in the future, your children might not have the same

opportunities to thrive, no matter how hard they work.

Why You Should Care: This is about fairness. It's about whether your hard work will get you ahead or the deck will always be stacked against you.

4. Your Mind Is Under Attack

Why It Matters: Social media is reshaping your brain, not in a good way. It's designed to keep you hooked, leading to depression, anxiety, and feelings of isolation, especially for young people.

- **Mental Health Crisis**: Teen depression and suicide rates are spiking, partly due to the toxic environment of social media, which exploits your emotions for profit.
- **Digital Overload**: We're now more connected than ever, but that constant connection is shortening attention spans, increasing stress, and reducing genuine human interaction.

Why You Should Care: This isn't just a problem for teenagers. It's affecting all of us. The time we spend online is taking a toll on our mental health and our ability to truly connect with others.

5. Democracy is Dying. Yes, Even in Your Country

Why It Matters: Authoritarianism is on the rise worldwide and creeping into democracies. Governments are becoming less transparent, elections are manipulated, and freedom of speech is under attack.

- **Elite Capture**: Corporations and the ultra-wealthy are buying influence in governments, effectively turning democracies into oligarchies. If you've ever felt your vote doesn't matter, this is why.

- **Surveillance States**: Even in supposedly free countries, surveillance and control are becoming normalized. This threatens your rights and freedoms in ways we've never seen before.

Why You Should Care: This affects your fundamental freedoms, your ability to speak your mind, access truthful information, and participate in free and fair elections. The health of democracy is the health of society.

6. Weapons of the Future Are Already Here, And They're Out of Control

Why It Matters: As governments invest more in military technologies, new weapons like autonomous drones and AI-driven arsenals are being developed and deployed without enough oversight.

- **Drone Warfare**: These "killer robots" are being used in conflict zones without public accountability, and they often target civilians.
- **Global Arms Race**: Trillions are spent on weapons every year, while healthcare, education, and social services go underfunded.

Why You Should Care: The unchecked use of these technologies threatens to destabilize entire regions, leading to more war and less peace. The money poured into arms could be spent on improving lives, not ending them.

7. The Future of Jobs is Bleak Unless We Act Now

Why It Matters: Automation and artificial intelligence are eliminating jobs faster than new ones are created, threatening the livelihood of millions. This isn't science fiction. It's happening now.

- **Job Loss**: Many jobs that used to support middle-class families are disappearing, and without serious intervention, millions will struggle to find work in the future.
- **AI Bias**: AI is making decisions about who gets a job, who gets approved for loans, and even who gets sentenced to prison. Often, these systems are biased against marginalized communities.

Why You Should Care: This isn't just about jobs disappearing. It's about how society will function if millions of people are left behind. AI can be a force for good, but only if we control it, not vice versa.

8. Climate Refugees Are Coming, and No One Is Ready

Why It Matters: As climate change accelerates, millions of people are displaced by rising sea levels, extreme weather, and drought. These "climate refugees" are already here, and their numbers will only increase.

- **Mass Migration**: Entire regions will become uninhabitable, forcing people to leave their homes for safety and stability.
- **No Protections**: International law still doesn't fully recognize climate refugees, leaving them vulnerable and without rights.

Why You Should Care: If we don't prepare for this now, the following humanitarian crises will affect everyone economically, politically, and socially. This is a global challenge we can't afford to ignore.

You Can't Afford to Ignore These Issues

These aren't distant problems. They're happening now and will shape the future for you and your loved ones. The more informed and engaged we are, the more power we have to demand change. The world is turning, and it's time to care about the issues that matter most.

Final Thought: A Call to Action

As you read this, it's easy to feel overwhelmed by the magnitude of our issues. It's easy to think these problems are too big, complex, or distant to make a personal difference. But the truth is, every one of us plays a role in shaping the world around us.

Imagine a future where our children and grandchildren look back on this time with disbelief that we allowed such crises to spiral out of control. Picture them asking why we didn't act when we had the chance. It's a sobering thought, but it's also a powerful motivator.

You can make choices that matter. You can educate yourself and others, support policies and practices that promote sustainability and fairness, hold leaders accountable and make personal changes that reduce your environmental impact. No matter how small, every action contributes to a larger movement for change.

The world is at a critical juncture, and our decisions today will determine the kind of world we leave behind. This isn't just about global issues. It's about your family, your community, and your own future.

Take a moment to reflect on what kind of legacy you want to leave. The power to change the trajectory of our planet is in our hands. Let's not squander this opportunity.

You matter. Your actions matter. It's time to be the change you wish to see. Act with urgency, compassion, and resolve. Together, we can confront these challenges and build a future that is not only sustainable but also just and hopeful. The world needs us to step up now more than ever.

www.ingramcontent.com/pod-product-compliance
Lightning Source LLC
LaVergne TN
LVHW091134080826
845145LV00008B/2151
* 9 7 8 1 7 3 9 2 1 2 9 2 6 *